DIGITAL NEUROMARKETING

THE PSYCHOLOGY OF PERSUASION IN THE DIGITAL AGE

SAM PAGE

TABLE OF CONTENTS

INTRODUCTION

In life, particularly in public life, psychology is more
powerful than logic.
~ Ludwig Quidde

Your brain isn't a computer.

I know we like to refer to our brains as computers. Computers have memories and so do our brains. We may jokingly refer to "searching through the files" when we're struggling to remember something. It's a convenient metaphor, but it's also completely wrong. Our brains are marvelously complex and endlessly compelling, but they are nothing like computers.

The Facts about Brains

Our brains are remarkable and often bizarre. They are unlike any other structure we know. Here are just a few of the things that make the human brain such a fascinating organ:

- The human brain contains, on average, 100 million neurons (nerve cells) and over a trillion synaptic connections between neurons.[1]

- The folds in the human brain mean that the brain has a much larger surface area than is immediately apparent. Each hemisphere of the human brain has a surface area of about 1.3 square feet.[2]

- The brain has 100 thousand miles of blood vessels and uses about 20% of all of the oxygen you take in.[3]

- Your brain is actually more active while you are sleeping than it is while you're awake.[4]

The brain is far and away the most complex organ in the human body. It's easy to understand why people want to compare it to a computer, but in fact, they are quite different.

The Differences between Brains and Computers

So how is your brain different from a computer? And is it in any way the same? Let's make a quick comparison:[5]

- Computers are ruled by logic. When you tell a computer to do something, it does it – provided you have used the proper commands and barring a mechanical malfunction.

- Brains are ruled by persuasion. The human brain is subject to a whole array of bizarre glitches and biases that override logic and even common sense.

- Computers access memory by referring to a precise memory address – a location in the computer where a particular memory is stored.

- Memories in the brain are linked to content. A simple memory -- such as the word for a familiar object – is linked not only to the verbal center of the brain but to sense memories and event memories.

- A computer has a fixed – and predictable – processing speed.

- The brain's processing speeds are unpredictable and difficult to pin down.

- Computers are organized according to their programming.

- Brains are self-organizing.

As you can see, the metaphor is not as accurate as you might have thought. Your brain is complex and so is a computer, but the similarities are mostly superficial. Sometimes when people put a digital marketing campaign together, they make the mistake of crafting the campaign for a computer instead of for the people in front of the computer. That's the difference between programming and persuasion – and that's what this book is about.

How Persuasion Works on the Brain

The goal of all marketing is persuasion, and the science of marketing psychology studies the ways that persuasion works on the human brain. I'll go into a lot of detail about this later in the book, but here are a few examples to whet your appetite.

1. A 1978 study at Harvard looked at conditions that would persuade people to agree to grant favors.[6] In the study, a volunteer asked to cut in line at a Xerox machine. To the control group, she said, "May I use the Xerox machine? I

only have five pages," and 60% of the people waiting agreed. To the experimental group, she said, "May I use the Xerox machine because I'm in a rush?" The number of people who were persuaded to allow her to cut in went up to 95% -- and all because she offered a reason for her request.

2. Our emotional reaction to loss is twice as intense as our emotional reaction to joy.[7] What that means in terms of persuasion is that if you want somebody to buy something, let them try it first. It's a cognitive bias known as *Loss Aversion*, and it's why companies give out free samples and free trial offers.

3. We use two different sets of criteria to judge our own behavior and the behavior of others, something known as the *Fundamental Attribution Error*.[8] What that means is that we excuse the things that we do while being quick to blame others. In terms of marketing, this is why so many addressing marketing content directly to the customer (by using "You") is very effective because it encourages the reader to be more lenient.

Those are just a few examples of how persuasion works on the brain, but the goal of this book is to go in-depth in discussing the art of persuasion as it relates to digital marketing.

What You'll Learn in This Book

When you're learning about any new topic, it's a good idea to start with the basics. In the first chapter, we'll talk about the fundamentals of marketing psychology. That includes explaining the fact that human beings have three brains -- something that might seem difficult to understand. In truth, it's simple, and by the time you're done with the first chapter you'll know exactly what that means. We'll also talk about cognitive biases and how they affect our decision-making process, as well as about behavioral psychology and the role it plays in marketing.

In the second chapter, we'll move on to one of the most important things for any marketer to understand, conversion rate optimization (CRO.) CRO is a way to increase your sales and conversions without spending more than you already are. It's a complex subject, but one we'll break down into easily understandable parts. Some of the topics we'll cover include Cialdini's Principles of Persuasion, the five cognitive biases you need to understand to increase conversions, and the importance of A/B testing individual components of your web page before making changes. Conversion rate optimization is a science, but it doesn't have to be an obscure one.

The third chapter's focus is on the psychology of web design. Web design encompasses a lot of different things, including the layout of your page, the colors and fonts you use, how users to your site find their way around, and the images and content you post. There's a hierarchy of web design, and it might surprise you to know that the aesthetics of your website are the least important thing about design. We'll talk about the things you need to focus on before you turn your attention to making things look good, including functionality and navigability. We'll also talk about the psychology of colors and fonts, and how even seemingly minor design choices can have a big impact on the way your customers perceive you.

In the fourth chapter, we'll go over another very important topic, persuasive writing. You probably remember having to do some form of persuasive writing in school, and with good reason. The ability to write persuasively is both an art and a science, and one that's particularly relevant to digital marketing. We'll talk about the components of a great headline, as well as how to write engaging emails that will pull your customers in and get them to convert. Effective persuasive writing isn't about using lofty language – it's about arousing emotions and promising solutions. I'll give you several psychological principles you can use to write headlines, emails, web content, and even calls to action.

The fifth chapter will build on everything that's come before it by talking about the psychology of paid advertising. Paid advertising is an essential part of any digital marketing campaign, and it can cover a wide variety of things. We'll start by talking about the psychology of search. How do people decide what to type into the search box on Google, and what are they expecting to find when they see the results? I'll explain why you need to look at a keyword as a question, as well as identifying the different types of keywords. From there, I'll tell you how to use Google AdWords effectively. After that, we'll go into one of the most effective forms of digital advertising, remarketing. We'll talk about when and how to use it, and which psychological triggers you can invoke to get customers to return to your website. Finally, we'll talk about social media advertising and why the rich psychographics you can use on Facebook make it easy to market to specific customer personas.

The sixth chapter is all about social media, and it in many ways encompasses all of the lessons of this book. Psychology is all about the self. Your customers are not interested in hearing about you or your product – they want to know what your product is going to do for them. Social media is the epitome of self-centered web activity. The majority of what users post on Facebook and Twitter relates to their personal experiences and emotions. Social media is not the place for an aggressive sales pitch, but it is the place for carefully-applied psychological marketing. We'll talk about the reasons people use social media, and the kind of content you should post. We'll also talk about some specific things you can do to build brand loyalty and a sense of community, including how to be true to your brand's personality.

The psychology of digital marketing might seem like an arcane topic, but the information in this book is designed to make it easy for you to understand and use. It will walk you through each topic in a straightforward way, and give you practical information and tips about how to apply each psychological principle to your own marketing campaigns.

As you begin reading, remember one thing. The focus of your marketing campaign, at every juncture, should be on your customers. Who are they? What do they want? What kinds of things will they respond to? What are their fears and desires? If you keep these questions in mind as you read, you'll be perfectly equipped to grasp the concepts being presented and to use them to increase your conversions.

Let's get started.

CHAPTER 1

MARKETING PSYCHOLOGY

The human brain is incredibly complex, and there's a lot we still don't know about it. When it comes to understanding how and why people make the decisions they make, researchers have just begun to scratch the surface. However, we are learning more every day about what makes people tick. While many of the applications of the ongoing research on the human brain relate to medicine, marketing researchers in the field of neuromarketing are making great use of psychology to make marketing campaigns more scientific – and more effective – than ever.

If you think about it, it makes sense. All marketing has the same goal – to get customers to make a decision in favor of a particular company or product. Understanding the decision-making process is absolutely essential, then, if you want to lead customers to a particular decision as quickly and efficiently as possible. As you might expect when talking about psychology, understanding has to begin with an examination of the human brain and how it works.

Beginning with the Brain

One of the most important things to understand – something that is the foundation of many of the principles of marketing psychology – is that human beings have what researcher Paul D. MacLean terms a triune brain.[9] That means that we have three different brains in one. Let's talk about what that means.

If you have even a rudimentary knowledge of Darwinism, you know that the human brain is the product of millions of years of evolution. All life on earth started in the sea, and we evolved over a long period. Some of the earliest creatures on earth were reptiles, and it turns out we still have something in common with them.

The first and most primitive part of our brains is called the reptilian brain. The scientific name for it is the basal ganglia, and it's the part of the brain that governs basic survival. It's the home of our fight-or-flight response – the thing that keeps animals alive in a life-or-death situation. According to Patrick Renvoise and Christophe Morin PhD in their book, "*Neuromarketing: Understanding the Buy Buttons in Your Customer's Brain*", this part of the brain, also called the old brain, actually plays a critical role in the decision-making process[10]. The reptilian brain is highly visual, and largely governed by fear.

The second part of the brain is the mammalian, or middle brain. This brain is also known as the limbic system, and it includes the septum, amygdala, hypothalamus, hippocampus, and cingulate cortex. This is the part of the brain that deals with our feelings, hormones, and moods. It also plays a significant role in decision making.

The third and final part of the brain is the most evolved part of the brain, the part that's responsible for rational thought and logic. It's called the human, or new, brain – the scientific name for it is the neocortex. It's also the place where our language skills and conscious thoughts live. We have a tendency to think that this is the part of our brain that makes decisions because it's the part that's capable of evaluating a product's features or price.

Influencing the Old Brain

All three of these brains coexist inside our heads, and research tells us that the key to influence resides in the reptilian brain.[11] Unless its fears and objections can be overcome, a customer is not going to take action and make a purchase. Once it moves from the reptilian brain, the decision still has to get past our emotions and moods before it can be addressed by the new brain.

Let's look at one way online marketers can overcome customer fear. Now, when you think of fear, you might be thinking of big things, true life-or-death situations like a plane crashing or a building burning. When it comes to human decision-making, though, fear is sometimes a lot smaller than that. For example, any purchase could be viewed as a risk because it involves a customer handing over money in return for an as-yet-untested product or service.

That basic fear is the reason you so often see marketing campaigns that offer subtle reassurances and guarantees. Look at this page from Defence Bank, and see how it works to alleviate customers' fears:

TAKE OUT A CAR LOAN AND
COMPREHENSIVE INSURANCE PACKAGE

6.69% pa **6.97**%* pa

Annual Rate   Comparison Rate

YOU COULD DRIVE AWAY WITH
$10,000 CASH#

Full competition terms and conditions
are available here.

ENQUIRE NOW
About a car loan

Note the two things I've outlined in green. The first is a display of three trust markers – symbols indicating awards the bank has won. The second is a comparison rate, which gives prospective customers a way to know what the total cost of their loan will be when they take all of the associated fees and charges into consideration. There's also an offer to enter a contest to win $10,000. The chances of any one customer winning are undoubtedly small, but the chance of winning something makes it easier for this web page to overcome fear and get customers to take the next step.

According to Renvoisé and Morin, the old brain can only be triggered by six stimuli[12]:

1- Self-centered

Robert Ornstein is a famous neuroscientist who stated that the old brain is the one that is in survival mode, so surviving is its only concern. In that regard, the old brain is very selfish.

With that said, it's important that the message you deliver is acceptable to the old brain of your customers. This means your message should be about your customers, not your products or services. They want to know you're on their side and that you care about their issues. Every visitor asks "what's in it for me?" This is because they care for themselves and their family.

Visitors to your website don't care about you, so don't waste words talking about yourself. Make it solely about the customer and what benefits you can offer them.

2- Contrast

The brain is attracted to things that are in contrast with each other. For example, things that contrast with something in the environment or previous events are fascinating to the reptilian brain.

The old brain looks for contrasts to make quick decisions and to avoid becoming confused, which happens when decisions are delayed.

Using a before and after photo comparison is a very popular technique, especially in the beauty and fitness industries. It can also be used to showcase a transformation of traffic, conversion rates, wealth, cleanliness, remodeling and so on.

The book, *Neuromarketing: Understanding the Buy Buttons in Your Customer's Brain*, states that the old brain is attracted to disruptions or changes. So using contrasts that show before and after, slow and fast, with and without, and risk and safety can help to highlight the features and benefits of your product in a way that appeals directly to the old brain.

To captivate your visitors, try to use contrast as a way to show the promise of your product or service.

3- Tangible

The old brain has a preference for things that are tangible. Promoting things like extra time and energy won't help you market to the reptilian brain. Instead, a better choice would be to discuss tangible benefits of using your product or service such as earning more money and increasing ROI.

4- Beginnings and Endings

The reptilian brain has a very short attention span, and it tends to do the best job remembering the beginning and end of whatever it hears. That means that when you're trying to sell to the old brain, it's important to start with a clear introduction that explains what you're offering, which is then followed by the body of your presentation and then finished with a conclusion (call to action). Any essential information must be repeated at the end if you want the old brain to remember it.

By ensuring a sequential flow for your content, you will enable your visitors to follow and pay attention easily. When your content is too complex, unclear or disjointed, then you will lose their interest rather quickly.

People are able to pay attention for about 10 minutes at a time, so every ten minutes, make sure you give them something emotionally stimulating to keep their focus.

5- Visual

The reptilian brain responds very quickly to visual stimulation. That doesn't mean that written content can't apply to the old brain, but it does mean that compelling visual content is your best tool for selling to the reptilian brain. Consider using photographs, infographics, illustrations and video to appeal to the old brain's preference for visual learning.

6- Emotion

Different emotions, including sadness, hope, excitement and anger, can be used in marketing to engage a customer and inspire them to take action. Shock is another great method to stimulate emotion. It's actually one of the oldest tricks in the advertising playbook.

"Emotion drives attention which drives learning." *Robert Sylwester, A Celebration of Neurons (1995)*

Your written and visual content should share the same emotion. If you can include emotion in both your images and written content, you can get people's attention with ease.

Influencing the Middle Brain

Once a web page has managed to satisfy the reptilian brain, it still needs to get past the mammalian brain – the home of emotion. Researcher Timothy D. Wilson of the University of Virginia did a study in 2005 that revealed that people make decisions based on something called affective predictions.[13] What that means is that they think about the emotional impact a future event – the result of a decision – will have on them, and they base their decision on their predicted emotions. It turns out we have a tendency to underestimate how quickly we'll recover from emotional impact, but that's actually something that can work in your favor when it comes to marketing.

The reason we overestimate emotional impact is due to our susceptibility to a cognitive bias – sort of a mental shortcut – called the impact bias. What's interesting about the impact bias is that it actually works in both directions. We overestimate the impact a decision will have on our future – something that marketers use when they show pictures of satisfied customers like this one:

It might seem simple, but an image like this one enables potential customers to envision themselves as part of that smiling group. In other words, it helps them to predict the impact of using this company's consulting services in a good way.

If – and only if – your marketing campaign can get past the defense mechanisms of the reptilian brain and the emotional concerns of the mammalian brain, it will finally reach your customer's neocortex – the new brain. That's when you can introduce information about pricing and features. If you bombard visitors to your site with that information right away, your page won't be effective. It's just that simple.

Avoid Doing these Things

Common mistakes people make that can hinder the old brain's decision-making process include the following:

- *Focusing content on your company or product, rather than on the needs of your target customer -- don't forget the old brain is self-centered.*

- *Not giving visitors clear contrasts that help to support your sales pitch -- contrast is very important.*

- *Leaving too much room for conception and thought --your message should be simple and tangible.*

- *Delivering content that is unnecessary and doesn't put emphasis on your selling points – your selling points should appear at the beginning and end of your content, and they should address pain and differentiate your claims.*

- *Using too many words, too often -- implement visuals throughout.*

- *Lacking emotion -- emotion helps draw in and inspire customers.*

There's a lot more to marketing than meets the eye, but hopefully this has helped clear up some of the mystery surrounding the human brain.

Influencing the Neocortex

Understanding the structure of the brain is important, but it's not the only thing you need to know about how to apply psychological principles to your website. One of the most important tools in the marketers' bag of tricks is having a working knowledge of cognitive biases. As I mentioned before, cognitive biases are mental shortcuts.

We are all susceptible to them, but one of the most fascinating things about our susceptibility is that we are largely unaware of it. In fact, these biases are so strong that we fall victim to them even when we know about them.

The rest of this book will have a lot of information about cognitive biases and how to apply them to digital marketing, but let's look at a couple of quick examples:

- The Decoy Effect is a cognitive bias that says that customers are willing to pay for a higher-priced product or service if a clearly inferior decoy option is included on the pricing page.[14] For example, let's say a business services company offered only two options, a basic and a premium option. They want people to buy the premium option, so they introduce an intermediate option that is close in price to the premium option but offers fewer benefits or features. The availability of the decoy increases the chance that clients will choose the premium option, even if they might otherwise have preferred the less expensive basic option.

- The Bandwagon Effect is a cognitive bias that makes us want to go along with the majority opinion. It originally applied to political campaigns, describing the tendency of undecided voters to vote for the frontrunner whether his platform aligned with their political beliefs or not.[15] It can be used by digital marketers in different ways, including finding ways to indicate a company's popularity by using statistics to imply that the majority of people use their services.

Those are just two cognitive biases to keep in mind, but there are dozens of them that have practical applications for digital marketing.

Behavioral Psychology

Another broad category of psychology that has applications in marketing is behavioral psychology. When a potential customer visits your website, there are certain things psychology lets us predict about their behavior. For example, we know that they will give more attention to the left side of a page than the right side,[16] which is why a lot of companies put their navigational tools there.

Behavioral psychology also indicates how a customer's eyes move over your website, how intently they read your content, and how quickly they get frustrated with a slow-loading web page – all things we'll talk about in greater detail later in the book.

Wrapping Things Up

The field of marketing psychology is a complex one. For marketers who don't have a background in psychology, it can be a lot to take in. The most important thing to remember is that the way people make decisions is not rational, although we have a tendency to think that it is. Our brains are extraordinarily complex, and it's not easy to craft a marketing campaign that will appeal to all parts of the brain. That said, it's not impossible, either. It requires an understanding of the triune structure of the brain, and a willingness to try different approaches until you find one that delivers the results you want. The information in this chapter is meant to serve as an introduction, but as we move forward you will learn about many additional principles that you can apply to your marketing campaigns.

Key Takeaways

The human brain is actually three brains in one:

- *The old, or reptilian, brain is the most primitive part of our brain, and its primary focus is on survival.*

- *The middle, or mammalian, brain is more evolved than the old brain, but still not particularly rational. Its primary focus is on emotion.*

- *The new, or human, brain is highly evolved and rational. Its primary focus is on evaluating quantifiable facts in a logical way.*

Any successful marketing campaign must address the fears of the old brain first. Some of the things to keep in mind include:

- *The old brain is selfish and me-centered. Your campaign should focus on the customer at all times.*

- *The old brain evaluates things through contrast.*

- *The old brain responds particularly well to extreme emotions like shock and fear.*

- *The old brain is highly visual and will process images much more quickly than it will words.*

- *The old brain prefers tangible benefits and rewards to intangible ones.*

- *The old brain remembers the beginning and end of a presentation, not the middle.*

After overcoming the objections of the old brain, you must address the emotional needs of the middle brain next. One thing to keep in mind is that people have a tendency to overestimate the emotional impact decisions will have on them.

A successful digital marketing campaign will avoid the following things:

- *Focusing on your company or product instead of the customer*

- *Failing to draw a clear contrast between the available options*

- *Allowing time for too much thought, or expecting rational thought to rule the day*

- *Providing content that is too long or fails to address the customer's fears*

- *Making significant points with words instead of pictures*

- *Presenting things in a dry, emotionless way*

Human beings are susceptible to a host of irrational decision-making shortcuts known as cognitive biases. Examples include the Decoy Effect and the Bandwagon Effect.

Behavioral psychology is also important in digital marketing, and helps marketers understand how customers process their websites. Examples include eye movement and focusing on certain parts of the page.

Now that we have laid down the foundation for understanding why psychology plays such an important role in your digital marketing efforts, it's time to go into the different aspects of digital marketing in depth. Our first topic will be one that every marketer should be concerned about – conversion rate optimization.

CHAPTER 2

CONVERSION RATE OPTIMIZATION

"It's much easier to double your business by doubling your conversion rate than by doubling your traffic."
~ Jeff Eisenberg

Any good digital marketer can tell you that digital marketing isn't one thing, it is many things. As a marketer, you've got to wear a lot of different hats. You're forced to think about everything from web design to product innovation and advertising strategies.

When you're wearing that many hats, it can be easy to get sidetracked. You might get caught up worrying about minute aspects of digital marketing, such as Search Engine Optimization or which font to use on your website. It's not that those things don't matter – they do! But the danger is that by focusing too much on individual details you can end up losing sight of the big picture.

When it comes to digital marketing, your goal, regardless of which aspect of marketing you're focused on, is to grow your business by increasing sales. That means that every single thing you do on the internet, from the keywords you choose to the design of your web pages, has to work toward helping you close more sales. That's where conversion rate optimization comes in.

What Is Conversion Rate Optimization?

Your *conversion rate* is the percentage of people who do what you want them to do after seeing your call to action. For example, if 5 of every 100 people who see your sales page buy your product, your conversion rate for that page is 5%. *Conversion rate optimization* is the process of optimizing a website, a landing page, or an ad with the intention of increasing its conversion rate.

Here's a quick overview of the conversion rate optimization process:

- You gather and examine data in order to understand your target audience better.

- You come up with a specific hypothesis that is based on that data, one that can be tested.

- You test your hypothesis, analyze the results, and implement changes if your hypothesis proves to be correct.

Let me give you an example. A company called Performable came up with the hypothesis that a page with a red "Get Started Now" button would perform better than their current page, which featured a green "Get Started Now" button. They tested their hypothesis and found that it was correct. Changing the button color from green to red increased their conversion rate 21%. That's a huge increase, one that indicates that the change is worth making.

Not every test you run will have that dramatic an impact. Most of your tests will yield small wins (less than a 10% increase in the conversion rate), and a few will yield big wins (more than a 10% increase in the conversion rate.) If you keep testing and improving your pages, small wins (3% here, 5% there) combined with an occasional large one will add up to big increases in your revenue.

Why Is Conversion Optimization So Important?

The importance of conversion rate optimization boils down to economics. When you conduct tests and make changes based on the results, you increase your sales without upping the amount of money you spend on advertising.

For example, if you sell a product that costs $25, and your conversion rate is 5%, it means that you make $125 in revenue for each 100 people that visit your website.

In order to increase your revenue you have to do at least one of these two things:

- Increase your traffic
- Increase your conversion rate

Targeted traffic (people who are interested in what you have to offer as opposed to those who just randomly stumbled upon your website) is expensive. To get more of it, you've got to spend your time and energy on free advertising, or spend your time, energy, *and* money on paid advertising.

Conversion rate optimization doesn't cost much, and if you've never put an effort into optimizing before, it's likely that you can substantially increase your revenue in a relatively short period of time. For example, if you could increase your conversion rate to 10%, instead of making $125 for each hundred people who visit your site, you'd be making $250 – without increasing your traffic.

It's important to note that increasing your conversion rate also means increasing the return on investment (ROI) on your advertising. In our example, running an ad campaign before doing conversion optimization would have gotten you $125 in revenue for every 100 people that visit your website. However, increasing your conversion rate from 5% to 10% means that the exact same ad campaign will now get you $250 in revenue for each 100 people who visit your website. You pay the same money for advertising, but when your site's optimized for conversion, you get better results.

As you can see, conversion rate optimization should be at the top of your to-do list if you want to increase your online sales.

The Science of Conversion Rate Optimization

It's important to understand that conversion rate optimization is a scientific method you can apply to every aspect of your digital marketing efforts.

As you begin the process of optimizing your page for conversions, it's important to remember that what you are doing is conducting a scientific experiment. Would a scientist skip gathering and analyzing the relevant data because he doesn't feel like it? Would a scientist draw conclusions from a sample of only five people? Would he stop an experiment before reaching statistical significance because the results seem obvious? He would not – and that means you shouldn't, either.

If that's not incentive enough, here's something else that should keep you on track. Unlike most scientists, you'll be conducting experiments with your own money. Straying from the scientific method and making sloppy mistakes could cost you tens or even hundreds of thousands of dollars in potential revenue. That's a lot of money to throw away by being careless – so don't be.

What Makes People Tick?

Some people see conversion rate optimization as a bunch of tricks, tests, and numbers. To them, it's all about button colors, capitalized words, and adding images in the right places. In other words, it's a collection of website hacks. Superficial changes like those might get you a small increase in your conversions in the short term, but in the long run, it's not the right approach to take.

To understand why, ask yourself this question:

What role does psychology play in conversion rate optimization?

Conversion rate optimization is all about persuasion – you want people to take a specific action, and you're trying to find a way to get them to do it. The secret to doing that is understanding these things:

- *Psychology of influence.* Your customers are prone to the same cognitive biases (mental shortcuts that influence decision-making) as everyone else. Understanding the psychology of influence will help you nudge them in the direction you want them to go.

- *Psychology of your target audience.* In addition to sharing common biases, your customers have a distinct set of psychological characteristics that you need to understand if you want to do a good job of selling to them. The more thoroughly you understand your target audience, the easier it'll be to get them to buy from you.

- *Psychology of design, content, marketing, etc.* What color scheme will appeal most to your customers? What kind of headlines will grab their attention? How should you craft your ads so potential customers will click through to your website? You need to know the answers to all of these questions if you want to run a successful digital marketing campaign.

As if all that weren't enough, there's one more thing you need to do to become skilled at conversion rate optimization. You've got to learn to resist the tendency to be overconfident about your predictions. We all do it, but assuming you know it all is a sure-fire way to fail. It's pretty common for marketers to talk about the importance of testing, but few people test their hypotheses as rigorously as they should. It's easy to rationalize your decision not to test when something seems obvious, right? But often, things aren't nearly as obvious as they seem. If you always trust your gut when making business decisions, you could end up losing a lot of money in the long run. Conversion rate optimization requires enough self-awareness to nip overconfidence in the bud.

In other words, the answer to the question "What does conversion rate optimization have to do with psychology?" is this: everything.

Our (Ir)Rational Decisions

We all like to think that we are rational people who make rational decisions. That is simply not true - and the sooner you let go of that idea, the better. Why?

There's a huge amount of research showing that our thought processes are riddled with bizarre mental glitches. Did you know that the weatherman is often blamed for bad weather? Or that tall men are more likely to get promoted? Or that the more attractive a presidential candidate is, the more likely he or she is to get elected? None of those things is based on logic, but that doesn't make them any less true.

If you're like most people, you're probably thinking, "I'd never fall for something like that. I make decisions based on logic." Everyone thinks that when they're first introduced to the research that supports our propensity for falling prey to such illogical thinking. But the reality is that if you're a human being, then you're susceptible to the same mental glitches as the rest of us, and you probably succumb to them on a daily basis.

What does all this have to do with conversion rate optimization? When you optimize your web pages for conversion, what you're doing is finding ways to use these quirks of human psychology to your advantage. Of course, you still have to make a solid case for your product or service on an intellectual level. But purchasing decisions are influenced by a wide variety of things, from the layout of your website to the particular words that you use to the color you choose for the "Add to cart" button. It's your job to figure out how to fine-tune each component of your page based on the applicable psychological research to convince more customers to convert.

Do you want to become good at conversion rate optimization? Let go of the myth that humans are rational animals. You're not rational – and neither are your customers.

So you better learn what makes them tick.

Six Principles of Persuasion

In 1984, Dr. Robert Cialdini published a book called "Influence: The Psychology of Persuasion." In that book, he took everything he learned during years of studying persuasion – both in the lab and in the field – and boiled it down to six key principles. Today, more than 30 years later, "Influence: The Psychology of Persuasion" is still considered to be one of the most important books about marketing ever written.[14]

As I mentioned earlier, conversion rate optimization is all about persuasion. How can you get your customers to click your ads, subscribe to your newsletter, and buy your products? Interestingly enough, Cialdini's principles are as powerful in terms of digital marketing as they were with traditional marketing. In fact, a lot of conversion rate optimization tactics are based on them. So let's take a closer look at each of the six principles of persuasion.

#1: Reciprocity

The principle of reciprocity states that people feel obliged to return favors even when doing so doesn't make sense. Have you ever invited someone you don't like to a party simply because they have invited you to a party before? It's obvious that this sense of obligation is irrational – after all, it's your party, so you're free to decide who gets invited and who doesn't – but the impulse to reciprocate is so strong that we'd rather put up with the company of someone we find annoying than resist the urge to return the favor.

One of the most famous experiments regarding reciprocity was conducted by psychologist Dennis Regan in 1971. The subjects of the study were asked to rate the quality of some paintings as part of an experiment in art appreciation. Each subject was paired with a guy called Joe, who they thought was another participant, but who in reality was Regan's assistant. With the control group, Joe left the room during the rest period, and returned empty-handed after the break.

However, with the experimental group, Joe left the room during the rest period and came back with two bottles of Coke, one for the subject, and one for himself. He'd say "I asked him (the experimenter) if I could get myself a Coke, and he said it was okay, so I bought one for you, too."

Later, after the paintings had been rated, and the experimenter left the room, Joe asked the subject to do him a favor. He'd explain to him or her that he was selling raffle tickets for a new car and that if he sold the most tickets, he would win a $50 prize. Then, Joe would ask the subject to buy some raffle tickets (for $0.25/ticket.) "Any would help," he'd say. "The more, the better."

The results yielded some interesting insights into the principle of reciprocity. Joe had a much easier time selling raffle tickets to the people for whom he had bought a bottle of Coke earlier. In fact, the experimental group bought twice as many tickets as the control group did.[15]

There was one additional finding in that study. Regan had the subjects fill out several rating scales that indicated how much they liked Joe and then compared the responses to the number of raffle tickets they bought from him. It turned out that that the more people liked Joe, the more tickets they purchased. Given what I've already told you about reciprocity, that information might not surprise you much, but here's the part that surprises most people.

Apparently, for the people who got a bottle of Coke from Joe, there was no correlation between liking him and buying raffle tickets. The subjects who disliked Joe bought as many tickets as those who liked him. Why? Because of the reciprocity bias. Regardless of whether they liked Joe, they felt obligated to return the favor he'd done them.

What are the implications of this finding for conversion optimization? What it tells us is that our impulse to reciprocate is so strong that it can overpower factors that normally lead to saying no. The people we dislike, such as annoying acquaintances and tiresome relatives, can increase the chances that we'll comply with their requests simply by doing us a small favor prior to making a request. That's a bit disturbing, isn't it?

Businesses can apply the principle of reciprocity by doing small unsolicited favors for potential customers before asking them to make a purchase. Companies have been doing this for decades, and non-profit organizations do it too. Have you ever gone to your mailbox and found an envelope from UNICEF or the World Wildlife Foundation? When you opened it, you probably found that they'd included a gift for you, usually a sheet or two of address labels for you to use. They always make a point of saying, in the enclosed letter, that the address labels are yours to keep whether you make a donation or not. A 2007 article in the Christian Science Monitor said that 70% of first-time donations come from people who received a free gift in the mail first.[16]

If you want to use the principle of reciprocity in your digital marketing, you have to give before you make any requests. If you do, when you make your offer, people will at least consider it.

For example, take a look at the home improvement superstore Home Depot. They make their money by selling home improvement supplies, everything from construction material to paint to gardening supplies. They also run a respected blog where they post tons of tutorials with step-by-step instructions for specific projects, all of which are available for free. Why would they spend time running a blog that requires a lot of effort yet doesn't make any money?

It's not out of the kindness of their hearts, at least not entirely. You see, by giving away valuable information for free, Home Depot builds credibility and trust. It ensures that if their readers are planning any kind of home improvement project, Home Depot will be the first company that comes to their minds. Who would you be more likely to trust, a company you have no personal connection to, or the one who's been giving you valuable blog posts about how to make your living environment more beautiful?

How To Install String Lights On A Porch

Posted by: Caitlin Ketcham on August 12th, 2015 | One Comment

Of course, not everybody who reads the blog will go on to shop at Home Depot, but the revenue that comes from the ones that do is more than enough to make the blog worth the effort.

This approach to creating and giving away content is called content marketing. Any business can use the same strategy. Do you own a bakery? Share your baking tips and tricks. Are you selling sports equipment? Post some videos on how to work out more effectively. Are you running a software company? Give people free advice related to the problem that your software solves. You get the idea. When you give valuable content away for free, the people who use it will be more likely to buy your product than they would if you gave them nothing.

One final note about content marketing. What you give away has to be valuable to your customers to be effective. Avoid posting promotional videos and keep your focus on what your customer needs, otherwise it won't work.

#2: Commitment and Consistency

The principle of commitment and consistency states that humans have a need to be consistent and are very likely to go through with something once we have made a commitment, even if we have doubts. Have you ever tried changing something about yourself that both you and others see as a part of your identity (religious beliefs, career, eating habits, etc.)? Then you know how hard it is to publicly change your mind. An experiment conducted by Tom Moriarty in 1975 is a good example of how powerful this particular bias is.[17] Here's how the study worked:

An accomplice of the researchers put a beach blanket close to a randomly-chosen individual who became the subject of the experiment. After a few minutes of sitting on the beach listening to a radio, the accomplice got up and went for a walk, leaving his radio behind. With the control group, the accomplice simply walked away without saying anything. With the experimental group, he turned to the person and asked them to watch his things while he was away.

A little while after the accomplice left, one of the researchers approached and tried to walk away with the radio. In the control group, only 4 out of 20 people made an effort to interfere with the robbery, while 19 out of the 20 who'd been asked for their help tried to stop the theft from occurring.

Commitment is the key here. The people in the experimental group were willing to risk their own well-being simply because they made a casual promise to a stranger. Moriarty's experiment proved that very few people are comfortable with the idea of breaking a promise.

Commitment is a dangerous beast. As soon as we publicly commit to something we are hard-wired to want to honor that commitment. Commitment doesn't have to mean making a promise to another person. It might refer to taking a stand on an issue, or even slightly leaning to one side or the other on a particular issue. The bias toward commitment holds even when it's not beneficial to us.

Let's look at a real-world example of how this particular principle is used. Many car dealerships employ a sales tactic called "throwing a low ball," which involves getting a customer to commit to an offer that is then rescinded. The dealer starts by offering a customer a great price – say, $1,000 below his competitor's price. Happy with the deal, the customer agrees to buy the car. He fills out forms and arranges financing. Sometimes the salesman will even let him drive the car for a day. All of the salesman's actions are carefully crafted to strengthen the customer's decision to buy that car.

Guess what? The dealer has no intention of selling the car at the price he quoted. Just as the customer is about to close the deal, something happens. The salesman's boss steps in and tells the buyer there's been an error in the calculations, and they can't offer the car at the price they quoted. He tells the customer they can still have the car, but they'll have to pay the extra $1,000 if they want it. The customer may be annoyed, but he tells himself that $1,000 is a drop in the bucket compared to the overall value of the car. Plus, as the salesman is quick to remind the customer, this is the car they chose, after all. More often than not, the customer buys the car at the higher price and drives away without ever realizing what happened.

How can you apply the same principle in your digital marketing campaigns? You do it by getting customers to make small commitments. Every time they make a decision in your favor, they become accustomed to seeing themselves as someone who's interested in what you're selling, and that makes them more likely to buy your product or service.

As an example, let's take a look at the home page of KissMetrics, a website performance tracking software. Do you see how they're emphasizing "Request a Demo" in their design?

When you click on "Request a Demo," you are redirected to a page where you have to fill out a form in order to request a one-on-one demonstration with a KissMetrics representative.

PERSONAL DEMO

Request a Personal Demo of Kissmetrics

WANT TO SEE HOW KISSMETRICS WORKS?
WE'D LOVE TO SHOW YOU.

Once you've filled out the form on the left, we'll reach out in the next couple of days and schedule a 1-on-1 demo with you.

Are you thinking that offering potential customers a personal demonstration seems inefficient? Maybe you think they should just put a demo video on their homepage.

The reason they don't use a demo video is because they understand how commitment and consistency work. When a potential customer takes the time to fill out the form, request a demonstration, and go through that demonstration, she is getting in the habit of making small commitments to KissMetrics. Those small commitments make her far more likely to sign up for the service that KissMetrics offers than she would be otherwise. After all, if she weren't planning to sign up, why would she have gone through all that hassle? The only behavior that's consistent with making those small commitments is to make the big one and sign up for the service.

To make this principle work for you, you don't need commitments that big. When you get people to read your blog posts, leave comments, subscribe to your newsletter, or email you, those are all commitments – and they all add up. They change the way customers perceive your company and themselves. The more small commitments they make, the more likely they are to buy from you when you make your offer.

#3: Social proof

The principle of social proof states that people tend to do what they observe other people doing in an attempt to behave correctly in a given situation. You know how teenagers all think they're different and misunderstood, yet they look and behave exactly as their friends do? The tendency to imitate the people around us never goes away.

One of the most famous experiments regarding social proof was conducted by psychologist Muzafer Sherif in 1936.[18] Here's how it worked:

Sherif placed the subjects in a dark room and asked them to look at a dot of light about fifteen feet away. The subjects were asked how much the light moved. The results varied from individual to individual but remained consistent for each person. (The truth was that the dot of light did not move but appeared to move due to an optical illusion.)

A few days later, the researchers divided the test subjects into groups of three and asked the same question again. Despite having come to different conclusions when they were questioned individually, each group came to a consensus about the movement of the light.

In the final phase of the experiment, the subjects were separated again and asked the same question one last time. Surprisingly, even though they were back to looking at the dot of light by themselves, they didn't revert to their original estimates. Instead, they gave answers that were close to the answer their group agreed upon, regardless of how different that answer was from their original estimate.

Our culture celebrates individualism, and we all like to believe that we're independent thinkers. However, countless experiments have shown otherwise, sometimes to the point of absurdity. When people see someone pointing at the sky, they stop and look at the sky themselves. If people find themselves in a room that's filling up with smoke, they stay in the room as long as the other people there ignore the smoke. When people see someone who's in an emergency situation and needs help, they don't do anything if others don't. It seems that we're less like snowflakes and more like sheep than we'd like to admit.

Our tendency toward social conformity can be used by businesses to influence customer behavior. For example, in 1934 an entrepreneur named Sylvan Goldman noticed that his customers would stop shopping in his grocery stores once their hand-held baskets became too heavy. He came up with a creative solution and invented the shopping cart.[19] When he introduced it, though, the shopping cart looked strange and unfamiliar, and puzzled customers continued to use the baskets instead. Goldman hired a few shoppers to use the carts in the store so that others could see how convenient his invention was. Soon everyone was using shopping carts, and Goldman's revenue skyrocketed. Eventually, Goldman went from being the humble owner of a few grocery stores to being a wealthy man – his net worth was over $400 million when he died.

How can you use the principle of social proof online? There are many ways to ensure your potential customers that you are the real deal. Anything that looks like an endorsement can be enough to do the trick if you're smart about it.

Customer reviews are one way to go about this. Think about the last time you bought something on Amazon. They put their reviews front and center – they're impossible to miss. You probably took some time to read the reviews, and the reviews affected your eventual decision to buy, right? Everyone does that – including your customers. Customer reviews are a must for any online store.

Customer Reviews

Testimonials are another good way to reassure your customers. Sure, testimonials are recommendations from strangers, but that doesn't mean they're not powerful. Take a look at AWeber, a company that provides email marketing software to help people to build and manage email lists. What do they have on their homepage? Testimonials from successful online entrepreneurs who have been using their services for years. That makes them look more credible in the eyes of potential customers.

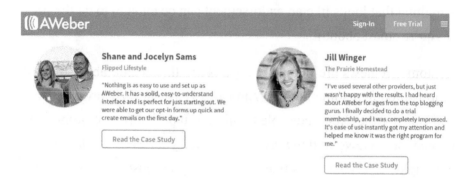

The testimonials are brief, but notice that in each case they also provide a link to a full case study. Case studies are even better than testimonials because they provide educational value.

It's important to understand that endorsements must be legitimate to be effective. Gone are the days when "This product is AMAZING!" - Jane Doe, Middle of Nowhere, US" could pass as social proof. Make sure your customers know that your endorsements are from real people or businesses.

#4: Authority

The principle of authority says that people, as a rule, are more likely to believe and trust information that comes from someone who they perceive to be an authority figure. This is a deep-seated preference that is probably a hold-over from childhood, when most of us grew up obeying our parents, teachers, and the other adults around us.

Stanley Milgram, a psychologist at Yale University, conducted an experiment to test how far people would be willing to go to comply with an authority figure.[20] In his lab, he paired each study participant with two people: an authority figure in a white lab coat, and another person who was hooked up to electrodes.

The person who was hooked to the electrodes was asked trivia questions. When they provided an incorrect answer, the authority figure told the study participant to administer a shock. (Note: The shocks were not real. The people hooked up to the electrodes were in on the experiment and they acted as if they had been shocked for the purposes of the study.) With each incorrect answer, the shocks grew stronger.

The results showed that a remarkably high percentage of study participants were willing to continue to administer the shocks even when the person answering the questions said they were in pain and asked them to stop. In fact, a full two-thirds of the participants continued to administer shocks all the way up to the highest level, which was 450 volts.

What does this mean for your digital marketing efforts? The study shows that the tendency of people to rely on advice from authority figures is very strong. One way to overcome the fears and doubts of potential customers is to use endorsements or recommendations from recognized authority figures in your industry. A single authority endorsement may be enough to sway a customer's decision.

#5: Scarcity

The principle of scarcity states that opportunities seem more valuable to us when they are less available. Think about your love life. Have you ever pursued someone who didn't seem interested in you? Or maybe someone you weren't interested in was crazy about you. What about the times you've played hard to get when you really were interested? That's the principle of scarcity in action – the less available something (or someone) is, the more interested we become. Conversely, the more available something or someone is, the more indifferent we are.

The principle of scarcity has many applications in business. If you can make your products seem like they're hard to come by, they will also seem more valuable. The Home Shopping Network and other television shopping channels use this tactic all the time. They start a promotion telling viewers that they only have a limited number of a particular item, and then they display a countdown as people starting calling in to buy it. When they do that, it creates a real sense of urgency that convinces people to pick up the phone and call so they don't miss out on a great deal.

How can you apply the principle of scarcity to your digital marketing? You can do it by displaying stock limits or time limits. What does that mean?

Let's use Booking.com as an example. They display the number of rooms that are available so that customers understand that they could miss out if they wait to book their stay.

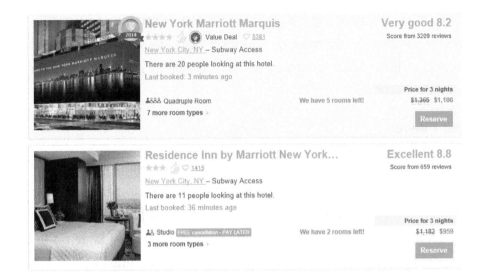

Let's look at another example. Woot.com is a site that sells a wide variety of products to consumers. Instead of counting the number of items available, they display an end date next to each deal. The end date adds a sense of urgency that customers might not feel without it. They look at it and think, I'd better hurry if I want to get that Roku 3 at a low price!

You can do the same thing with your products or services. Either offer a limited amount of products or offer a deal that runs for a limited period of time. It's a great way to make people reach for their credit cards!

#6: Liking

Okay, so the last principle is not going to be a surprise to anyone – the more we like someone, the easier it is for them to persuade us to comply with their requests. Have you ever done a favor for someone you had a crush on, helped a friendly coworker, or left a large tip for a cute waitress? All these people have one thing in common: you like them. Let's talk about the three main factors that make us like another person.

Physical attractiveness

We find it easier to like people we find attractive, largely because of a cognitive bias known as the *Halo Effect*. The halo effect says that an observer's overall impression of a person, company, or product influences the observer's feelings and thoughts about specific properties and characteristics of that person. When it comes to physical attractiveness, it means that someone who is physically attractive is likely to be perceived as being interesting, intelligent, and kind, as well.

In 1972, Dion, Berscheid, and Walster studied the Halo Effect. 60 students, 30 male, and 30 female, participated in the experiment.[21] Each subject was given three different photos to examine: one of an attractive person, one of an average person, and one of an unattractive person. Then, they were asked to evaluate the people in the photos in several different ways:

- The rated the people on 27 different personality traits (including altruism, trustworthiness, kindness, etc.)

- They were asked to approximate the overall happiness that the people would feel for the rest of their lives, including social happiness, professional happiness, marital happiness, and family happiness.

- They were asked whether they thought they people in the photos held jobs of low status, medium status, or high status.

What were the results? Participants believed that attractive people were more altruistic, trustworthy, kind, etc., that they held higher status jobs, and that they were happier overall than less attractive people.

One way that companies use the Halo Effect regularly is by getting well-liked celebrities to endorse their products. If you remember the old Vicks 44 commercials, the ones that featured an actor saying "I'm not a doctor, but I play one on TV" you know what I'm talking about. A more recent example comes from skin care company Aveeno. They feature actress Jennifer Aniston in television commercials and on their website. The actress's likability and beauty transfers to the product.

Similarity

The next thing that makes us like people is this: we like people who are similar to us. It doesn't matter much what kind of similarity it is – it can be background, fashion sense, political views, personality traits, etc. People say that opposites attract, but in reality, it's similarities that attract.

If you think about your own life, you'll realize how true this is. Aren't you more likely to help someone who's dressed like you are than someone who's not? You'd probably rather buy insurance from someone who's your age, or who has a similar background than from someone whose background is alien to you. A 1965 study by Timothy Brock demonstrated how this particular bias works.[22] The study looked at customers buying paint and found that they were more likely to buy paint from a salesperson who claimed to have a similar need for paint than from a salesperson who didn't. The bias toward similarity held true even when the salesperson claiming similarity had far less experience than the other salesperson.

How can you apply this online? Well, the best way to do that is to give your company a face so that people think of a particular person when they think about your company. And, of course, make sure that the person that is the face of your company shares a lot of similarities with your target customers. This principle is a little different from the Halo Effect, because its goal is to get your customers to identify with the person who's the face of your company, not to attribute their good qualities to your product or service.

One good example is Empire Flippers, an online marketplace where you can buy or sell an online business. Justin and Joe, the owners of Empire Flippers, run a free weekly podcast in which they give advice on building and selling websites. The podcast is informative, but also casual, personal, and fun, which makes the listeners like them. After all, Justin and Joe are entrepreneurs just like them. If a listener decides to buy or sell a website where do you think they'll go? To the website brokers they like and trust, Justin and Joe.

Founders

Justin Cooke
Founder

Joe Magnotti
Founder

One way to use similarity on your website is to find ways to inject some personality into your pages. For example, does your "About" page make your team look like real people or like corporate cyborgs? Are the articles on your blog engaging or boring? Consider making a video featuring you or your employees, or starting a podcast. Don't be afraid to show your customers that you and your team are people just like them.

Keep in mind that you should always consider your target audience. For example, a video show in which you casually talk about business dressed in a T-shirt, shorts, and flip-flops might work well if your audience is independent entrepreneurs, but the same approach would be disastrous if you run a law firm. You've got to make sure your customers see both your content and your tone as appropriate.

Compliments

We like people who like us. After all, everyone wrestles with doubts and insecurities from time to time, and it feels great to get some reassurance from others. That's why praise is such an effective persuasion tool.

What's interesting is that we seem to fall for compliments even when we know that the person flattering us has his own motives. There was an interesting experiment done by Martin and Wilson that showed that Millennials (people born between 1982 and 2000) were highly aware of the effects that paying compliments (identified in the study as brown nosing) had on their ability to get ahead.[23] The research suggests that paying compliments (and our susceptibility to them) is less a cognitive bias and more a cultural phenomenon. Most of the students were able to identify brown nosing behavior, but they acknowledged that it was useful in particular situations.

Compliments can be used to get more sales. For example, Joe Girard, who was known as the world's greatest car salesman, said that his secret was getting customers to like him. How did he do that? Well, the fact that he sent his 13,000 customers a greeting card with the phrase "I like you" on it *every month* might have had something to do with it. There was nothing on the card except that phrase and Joe's name. "I'm just telling 'em that I like 'em," explained Joe. It must have worked, because Joe was selling an average of four to five cars a day and making hundreds of thousands of dollars every year.

How can you apply this to your digital marketing? You can start by congratulating customers on small wins. For example, take a look

Memrise, a company that sells flashcard software. Every time you remember a piece of information, say, how to say "Hello" in Spanish, you get points. When you collect enough points, you get a badge of honor, and if you make it to the Top 10 in a particular course, Memrise will send you an email and congratulate you on your achievement. That might seem a little silly to you, but the constant high-fives from Memrise are one of the things that make people complete courses like "The 5000 Most Common Spanish Words."

Take a look at your website. At what points should you congratulate people on small wins or thank them for their time and attention? Remember, compliments go a long way, so even a simple "Thank you, you're awesome!" when they confirm their email subscription can have a big impact. Shower your customers with affection and they will like you more.

If you use these six basic principles of persuasion effectively, you can move your customers through your sales funnel quickly, and watch your conversion rates go through the roof.

The bizarre world of cognitive biases

We talked briefly before about cognitive biases, but let's go into a bit more detail now. Cognitive biases are mental shortcuts we all use -- tendencies to think in certain ways that can lead to systematic deviations from a standard of rationality or good judgment. They're especially interesting to psychologists, economists, and marketers.

Here are five cognitive biases that you need to be aware of when it comes to conversion rate optimization:

#1: Anchoring

Anchoring is a human tendency to rely on the first piece of information (the "anchor") when making a decision even if that piece of information is obviously wrong and/or completely irrelevant to the decision in question.

An experiment that was conducted by Dan Ariely, George Loewenstein, and Drazen Pelec is a great example of how anchoring looks in practice.[24]

In the study, researchers presented six products (computer accessories, wine bottles, luxury chocolates, and books) to 55 students from Pelec's marketing research class. After briefly describing each product, they asked the students to write the last two digits of their social security number on a piece of paper. Then, they asked the students if they'd be willing to pay that many dollars for the items presented earlier. Lastly, the researchers asked the students to write down the maximum price they would be willing to spend on each item.

When Ariely asked the students whether they thought that writing down the last two digits of their Social Security number influenced how much they were willing to pay, they immediately dismissed the idea. However, when the researchers analyzed the results, it became clear that it had a massive impact. The students who wrote down the lowest numbers (00 to 19) were the lowest bidders. The students who wrote down the highest numbers (80 to 99) were the highest bidders, and were willing to pay an average of $198 for the items on the offer, which was *three times* as much as the lowest bidding group.

You can use the anchoring effect in digital marketing by giving your customers a base rate value to attach to your product or service. Let's look at an example. ConvertKit is a company that provides email marketing software that's more expensive than the software provided by their main competitors MailChimp (free) and AWeber ($19/month). So how do they get people to pay a higher rate? Look at how their pricing page is designed:

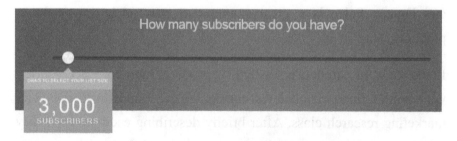

For up to 3,000 subscribers you'll pay $49 per month.

Create your account

They anchor the price at \$49 per month, but let visitors to the site choose the number of subscribers they have. Most small businesses have fewer than 3,000 subscribers, so they scroll back. When they do, the lowest rate of \$29 per month doesn't seem that expensive, even though compared to other email marketing software providers, it is.

You should anchor your prices in a way that makes them seem reasonable. Always offer several pricing options so that people are comparing your prices to one another, not to the prices of other companies. Then, put emphasis on either the middle or the most expensive option, so that it acts as an anchor.

#2: Loss Aversion + #3: Framing effect

Loss aversion is the strong tendency to prefer avoiding losses to acquiring gain. The framing effect is the tendency to react to a particular choice in different ways depending on how it is presented. These two cognitive biases often go together because people framing something as a gain or as a loss has a drastic effect on the way people perceive it.

An experiment conducted by Amos Tversky and Daniel Kahneman in 1981 is a great example of both loss aversion and the framing effect.[25]

In their study, they presented two different options for treating a disease that had infected 600 people. In the first frame, they told participants that Option A would save 200 lives while Option B had a 33% chance of saving everybody and a 66% chance of saving nobody. That's the positive frame, and study participants overwhelmingly chose the first option with its promise of saving 200 lives.

In the second frame, they said that Option A would kill 400 people, and that with Option B there was a 33% chance that all 600 people would live and a 66% chance that all 600 people would die. That's the negative frame. Presenting the information this way made most participants select Option B instead of Option A.

Note that the effectiveness of the treatments didn't change. Regardless of the frame, the outcome of the treatments is the same in both frames. However, treatment A was chosen by 72% of participants when it was framed positively and by only 22% when it was framed negatively. It's clear that the exact same information can be perceived very differently depending on the way it's framed.

Let's look at an example from insurance carrier AIG. This is from the page focusing on their accident and health insurance. They've framed it negatively by saying "Accidents happen when you least expect them."

Accidents Happen When They're Least Expected...

Instant Coverage. Guaranteed. No Medical Exam.

It's a fact of life: Accidents happen, often when we least expect them. Car wreck on the freeway. Fall from a ladder at home. Mishap with work machinery. What if one of these common accidents happened to you?

Accidental Death and Dismemberment Insurance from AIG Direct can help offset the financial burden your family might face in the event of your injury or death in an accident.

Instantly Help Protect Your Family* in just a few clicks...

GET COVERED ONLINE NOW >

The negative frame helps push customers toward a purchase of insurance because it makes them worry about what would happen to their families if something happened to them. Notice how AIG mitigated the negative framing a bit by showing a picture of a happy family? That's very effective because it shows potential customers what they have to lose.

#4: Illusion of truth effect

The illusion of truth effect, also known as the illusory truth effect or the truth effect, is the tendency to believe information to be correct because of the repeated exposure to it. The effect was first named and defined after an experiment conducted by Hasher, Goldstein, and Toppino in 1977.[26]

In the study, subjects were given a list of 60 factoids that seemed plausible ("The first air force base was launched in New Mexico", "Large migration of Chinese railroad workers began in the 1880s", "Basketball became an Olympic discipline in 1925", and so on.) They were asked to rate their belief that a particular statement was true on a scale from one to seven.

The experiment was repeated three times with two weeks in between each session. One-third of the statements remained the same in all three lists while the rest of the statements were new on each occasion.

The researchers found that repeated exposure to a statement increased the level of belief in it. Subjects rated repeated statements higher each time: 4.2 in the first session, 4.6 in the second session, and 4.7 in the third session. There didn't seem to be any patterns in the rating of the rest of the statements.

How can you apply this principle online? Have a clear message and repeat it every chance you get. The more you expose your customers to your message, the more they will believe in it. Some examples of how to do this include:

■ Using a long-form landing page with multiple testimonials or calls to action

■ Setting up an email campaign where you send out repeated emails about a particular product

■ Retargeting customers who've visited your site without making a purchase

Keep in mind, there's a fine line between repeated exposure and spamming. Don't keep sending your customers the exact same text. Mix things up by phrasing it differently while still conveying the same message.

#5: Von Restorff effect

The Von Restorff effect is the tendency to remember an item that stands out like a sore thumb better than all the other items.

This effect is named after psychiatrist and pediatrician Hedwig von Restorff, who conducted a series of memory experiments in 1933. During her most famous experiment, she asked the subjects to memorize a list of ten items, in which nine of the items were written in black ink, and one was written in blue ink.[27] Guess which item the subjects remembered the best? Of course, the one written in blue ink, which stood out like a sore thumb.

Understanding the Von Restorff effect is especially important in web design. For example, remember that test Performable ran where a change in button color ended up increasing their conversion rate by 21%? It's tempting to interpret those results in a simplistic "Red is better than green" manner. But the reality is that it wasn't the magical properties of the color red that increased the conversion rate – it was the fact that, in that particular color scheme, the color red stood out. Look at this example from WebDAM. Visitors to their site can't miss that bright orange button. That's the Von Restorff effect in action.

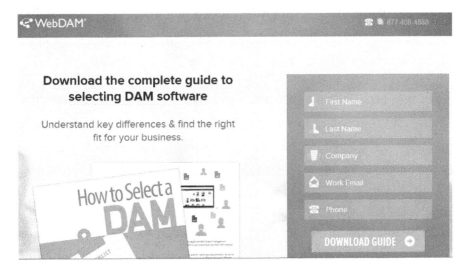

What stands out gets clicked, and what blends in goes unnoticed. If you want your customers to pay attention to a particular element of your web site, make sure that element stands out.

Paradox of choice

One last thing that you should be aware of when it comes to conversion rate optimization is the so-called paradox of choice. We are used to thinking that having more options is preferable to having few options. However, the research seems to indicate that often, the exact opposite might be true.

The most famous experiment on this is the study conducted by Mark Lepper and Sheena Iyengar in 2000.[28]

The researchers set up a display of exotic jams in a gourmet store, offering free samples and giving customers a coupon for a dollar off if they bought a jar. In one condition of the experiment, six varieties of jam were available for tasting while 24 varieties of jam were available for purchasing. In another condition of the experiment, all 24 varieties of jam were available for tasting, as well as for purchasing.

The large array of jams attracted more people to the table than the small array of jams. However, when it came to actually making a purchase, only 3 percent of people who were exposed to 24 varieties bought a jar, as opposed to 30% of those who were only exposed to 6 varieties of jam.

This study demonstrates the paralyzing effect a variety of choice can have on people. Making a decision is a draining task – and the more options you have to evaluate, the harder that task becomes. That's why the more options you give to people, the more likely they are to do nothing.

You want people to take action? Then, in general, it's better to provide the smallest number of options possible. Each page on your website should have *one* clear goal, and anything that doesn't serve that goal must go. Otherwise you're just distracting your customers and inducing choice paralysis.

For example, Taloon.com, an e-commerce store that sells hardware, increased the conversion rate of their product page by 11.9% by removing social media buttons. It's not that social media isn't important, but if the buttons aren't nudging your customers toward the main goal of that page, then they've got to go. Don't be afraid to kill sacred cows when it comes to reducing choice and distractions.

Of course, it's also important to apply some common sense. In certain situations, providing options might help you increase your conversion rate. For example, three pricing plans are usually better than one because that way you can anchor the price any way you want. Just try to keep the number of options under control – any more than three will probably confuse your customers.

There are dozens of cognitive biases that have been identified by psychologists and researchers. The few that I've outlined here are some of the most effective biases when it comes to influencing consumer behavior. They're easy to use, and the applications in marketing are clear. If you use them appropriately, they can make a huge difference in your conversion rate.

Gathering and Analyzing Data

When it comes to doing online testing, the number of things you can analyze is enormous – everything from page layout to headlines to button colors. Because of that, haphazardly testing random things in hopes of hitting a big win is like going through a haystack in hopes of finding a needle. It's a waste of time, energy, and money.

So how do you cut through that haystack? You do it by taking the time to gather and analyze data that allows you to understand your customers better. Then you'll be able to come up with hypotheses that are worth testing.

Here are three ways to gather and analyze data to help you understand your customers better:

Google Analytics

Google Analytics is a great way to gather quantitative data about how people are using your website.

Its most valuable feature when it comes to conversion rate optimization is its ability to track the performance of your *sales funnel*. Your sales funnel is the series of steps that a potential customer must take to go from arriving at your website to completing a purchase. For example:

- Click on search engine ad

- Watch video on landing page

- Sign up for mailing list

- Receive email highlighting product

- Click on link

- Buy product

That's a simplified example, but Google Analytics can show you the conversion rate of each step in your funnel. The data you collect allows you to identify and fix leaks in your sales funnel. For example, if you notice that your sales page has a high bounce rate, you can split-test purchasing options to identify the issue. That's valuable information, and every company that's involved in digital marketing should be using Google Analytics.

Surveys

Surveys are a great way to gather qualitative data and gain valuable insights into how your customers think. There are two types of surveys that you might want to conduct:

1. On-site surveys focus on people who are currently on your website. Your aim with on-site surveys should be to find out what's preventing people from buying. Are they confused about something? What reservations do they have? What is preventing them from making a purchase right now?

2. Customer surveys focus on people who have already bought your product or service. Your aim with customer surveys should be to find out what made them buy your product. What other options did they consider? What made them choose you over other options? What ultimately convinced them to buy?

The most important thing when it comes to surveys is asking open-ended questions. So, for example, a good question for an on-site survey might be "Is there anything preventing you from placing your order today?" Meanwhile, a good question for a customer survey might be "Why did you decide to choose us over the other options?" *Yes* and *No* answers won't help you get at the heart of your customers' behavior. Give people an opportunity to talk about their experiences in their own words

Once you have gathered enough data (the absolute minimum is ten answers, but ideally, you should wait until you have 100+ answers), it's time to analyze it, looking for patterns:

- *Objections.* What are the reasons for not buying (or almost not buying) that keep coming up over and over again? You need to address those things on your website if you want to dispel the reservations that people have and push them over the fence.

- *Reasons for buying.* What do people say when asked why they made a purchase? Is it because of the price? Or is it because of a particular feature, or because they trust your brand? Take note of all of these things so you can emphasize them on your sales page.

■ *Language.* Lastly, pay close attention to the language your customers use, because it's the language in which you need to communicate with them. What specific words and phrases do they use to explain their reservations, their reasons for buying the product, and their happiness about the purchase? These are the words and phrases you should use on your sales page.

All this qualitative data will help you understand what your customers *really* think. You might be surprised by what you can learn when you let your customers talk and listen to what they have to say. Here are some sites to consider using to set up surveys:

Survey Monkey

Polldaddy

Zoomerang

Survey Gizmo

Usability tests

Usability tests are a great way to identify issues that might be preventing potential customers from making a purchase. They're relatively simple to conduct. You ask people to use your website in a specific way (say, to purchase your product), and get them to share their comments as they go. You should also record their computer screen and their comments during the test.

Ideally, you should get people who are in your target audience to test your website, but often even those who are not potential customers can point out sources of confusion. You can ask your family, friends, or even strangers at a coffee shop to help you out with this (you only need around ten tests to identify the main issues.) You also have the option of getting a company that specializes in user testing to conduct tests for you.

Usability tests are valuable because they help you identify problems that you can't see because you're too familiar with the way things are supposed to work. For example, you might think that your check-out process is as straightforward as it gets, but your users might find it confusing. This kind of issue is easy to catch and simple to fix, but if it goes unnoticed, its impact on your conversion rate might be devastating. Here are some usability testing companies to consider if you don't want to conduct the tests yourself:

Ovologger

UserTesting

Userlytics

The more data you collect from your customers, the better able you will be to understand who they are, and why they make the decisions they do. Get a combination of quantitative and qualitative data for the best results. When you have enough data, you can move on to the next step, which is creating a customer persona.

Creating a Customer Persona

A customer persona is a customer archetype that's based on the data you have gathered. It represents who your buyers are, what they're trying to accomplish, and what drives their buying decisions.

Take a look at these buyer personas that a company called MailChimp came up with after analyzing their data:

You might be wondering: why would anyone bother creating these customer personas? Why not just use the data that backs up the personas? Well, we're used to interacting with other humans, not with nebulous things like target demographics. Creating a customer persona helps you boil all those numbers and survey answers down to an archetypal image that you can relate to.

Take a look at the data you've gathered. Who are your customers? What's their average age? Are more of them a particular gender or nationality? Why do they buy your product? What's the problem they're trying to solve? As you answer these questions, a customer archetype (or two, or three) will emerge. That's the customer persona that will help you improve your conversion rate.

Keep in mind that all your customer personas must be based on customer research. That means with each statement you include in your customer persona, you should be able to point to the data that supports that statement. Customer personas are only useful when they're grounded in reality.

There's No Such Thing as Too Much Information

You might be wondering how much data you should collect prior to testing. I'd recommend letting Google Analytics run for at least a month, getting at least 100 survey responses, and having at least ten people test your website before you start running tests. It's important to understand that, provided you're tracking relevant metrics, there's no such thing as too much information. More data means clearer patterns and more accurate conclusions, so when in doubt, gather more information.

Coming Up with a Hypothesis to Test

People often conduct tests in hopes of stumbling across a big win. You know what industry experts call that? Spaghetti testing. That's not conversion rate optimization; it's throwing spaghetti at the wall to see if it sticks. You need to form a clear hypothesis prior to running a test if you want to do actual conversion optimization. How do you do that?

Step #1: Understand what you're optimizing for

Obviously, the ultimate goal of every business is to increase profits, but that doesn't mean that every page of your website should be aimed at making sales. Instead, your goal should be to get the potential customer all the way through your sales funnel, one step at a time. That means that each page should be optimized for nudging the customer to proceed to the next step.

Keep in mind that each page on your website should have *one* clear purpose, whether it's to get people to sign up for your email newsletter, or to click through to a pricing page, or to click the "Buy now!" button and complete the purchase.

Step #2: Pick a specific problem

Once you understand the purpose of a particular page, it's time to pick a specific problem that you want to address.

For example, maybe you've decided that the goal of your homepage should be getting people to sign up for your newsletter, but people are bouncing away instead of subscribing. That's a good thing to test. When you have a specific problem to solve, it's easier to form a solid hypothesis.

Step #3: Come up with a hypothesis

Now it's time to put your knowledge of psychology and your understanding of your customers to work. You have a specific problem that you need to solve. What's the best way to do that?

For example, if you want people to sign up for your newsletter, you might try using the principle of reciprocity. You could offer them a free video series or a short eBook as an incentive to sign up for your newsletter. In that case, your hypothesis would be, "Offering customers a gift will incentivize them to subscribe to my list."

Keep in mind that your hypothesis must be grounded in something more substantial than your gut feeling. Why do you think this particular solution will work? You have to be able to give a clear answer to that question.

<u>You must test the hypotheses!</u>

Sometimes, people who've put a lot of thought into their hypothesis are tempted to skip testing it because they're sure their hypothesis is correct. After all, if you can point to the data that supports it, then there's not much point in testing it, right? Wrong!

That's not how science works. It doesn't matter how obvious something seems to you. You won't know for sure unless you run a test. Never give in to the temptation to skip testing a hypothesis.

Remember, you're not playing some game where you tweak stuff based on hunches, you're conducting scientific experiments that can have a real impact on your revenue – so act like it.

A/B Testing the Hypothesis

This section will explain how to test the hypotheses you have come up with regarding the performance of your sales funnel. Testing isn't complicated – there are plenty of tools to help you do it – but it's important. If you do it properly, it can have a big impact on your conversion rate.

What is A/B testing?

A/B testing (also known as split testing) is a process during which you test two different versions of a page against one another. The "A" page is your control page, and the "B" page is your experimental page. The goal is to determine whether a specific change in your existing page will increase your conversion rate.

For example, if you want to see whether offering a free video series will get you more email subscribers, then you test the current version of your homepage (A) against a version of your homepage in which you offer a free video series (B). You can use software to send 50% of your traffic to page A and 50% of your traffic to page B, and compare the results.

A/B testing is extremely valuable because it allows you to test your hypotheses and get clear answers.

Your first A/B test

The term "A/B testing" might sound intimidating, but in reality, running these tests is quite straightforward. Here are the basic steps to follow:

Step #1: Choose the software

There are quite a few companies that offer reliable A/B testing software, but I recommend you start with one of these three options:

Google Analytics – Google Analytics is free, and you can use their "Content Experiments" feature to split-test your website. However, it's not the most user-friendly option, and if you're not an experienced analyst, it might not be the best choice. If you're comfortable with Google Analytics already, you might want to give it a try before paying for a service.

Optimizely – Optimizely is reasonably priced, and offers options for split testing, multivariate testing (testing more than two options), and mobile testing. The interface is intuitive, and you can always upgrade to more comprehensive options as your sales increase. The downside is that the data won't be integrated with Google Analytics, but it's a good option to start with.

Visual Website Optimizer – VWO is more expensive than Optimizely, but it also offers some really nice features, including an idea generator if you're not sure what elements of your website to test.

The most important thing is choosing software that makes it easy to run A/B tests. Check out the options above and pick the one that you find the most appealing.

Step #2: Set up the test

The next step is setting up the software to test the current version of a page (A) against the new version of that same page (B).

The how-to is different for each program, so if you're not sure how to do it, check out the tutorials for the specific software that you are using.

Step #3: Run the test

Once everything is set up, all you need to do is press a button, and your A/B test is running. Simple, right? Well...

This is where a lot of people mess things up. There's a thing called statistical significance that shows how likely it is that one variation is a winner. The problem? People often stop the test before reaching an appropriate level of statistical significance, and that renders the test results useless.

Most experts run a test until they reach 95% statistical significance. At that point, the likelihood that the test results are a fluke is very low, and therefore it's reasonable to draw conclusions from the results. Stopping the test before that means that the data you collect is skewed by random factors, which means that there's not much connection between the changes you made and the results you got. What's the lesson here?

Keep running the test until your software shows that you've passed the threshold of 95% statistical significance.

Okay, so you have your results, now what?

Let's say you ran the test, you did it properly, and you're sure that the results are accurate. What should you do now?

The answer is pretty straightforward. You'll do one of two things:

- **Your hypothesis was incorrect, and your control page won.** That means that it's time to go back to the drawing board.

What else can you do to increase the conversion rate of that particular page? If you tested a particular gift to incentivize people to sign up for your list, you might want to test another gift or try tweaking other aspects of your page, such as the form you're asking people to complete to subscribe.

- **Your hypothesis was correct, and your experimental page won.** That means it's time to ditch the control version of the page and replace it with the experimental version. Congratulations!

It's important not to be lazy about implementing what you've learned. Let's say your experimental page won by a small percentage, for example, 3%. Is it worth to make the changes for such a small gain? The answer is yes. Big wins are rare. Most tests are going to lead to small gains such as 1%, 3%, 5%, etc. Don't scoff at these numbers, because they add up over time. Just keep implementing what you learn.

5 Most Common A/B Testing Mistakes

A/B testing is relatively straightforward, but new marketers and entrepreneurs mess it up all the time. You don't want to make the mistakes that they do, so let's go through them so you can avoid them.

#1: Testing more than one variable at a time.

People sometimes try to improve conversions faster by testing several variables at the same time. For example, they might change the color of a button and change the text on the button as well. The problem with this approach is that it's difficult to draw any conclusions from a test like that. Your conversion rate may have increased, but was it because of the change in button color, the change in button text, or a combination of both? There's no way to know without running more tests.

Remember that A/B testing is about testing only *one* variable at a time – adding more variables ruins the test unless you are actually conducting a multivariate test, which I don't recommend until you have mastered A/B testing.

#2: Stopping the test before reaching 95% statistical confidence.

Yes, I know, I'm repeating myself, but this is extremely important. Stopping the test before reaching an appropriate level of statistical significance – 95% -- means ruining the entire test. Can you afford to waste time, energy, and money on tests that provide no value to you? Probably not. I'll talk a little later on about what to do if you're not getting enough traffic to reach statistical significance, but as a rule, it's best to keep running the test until you get to 95%.

#3: Running the test for less than a week.

Conversion rates often vary depending on the day of the week. That means that you have to run each test for at least a week, even if you reach 95% statistical significance sooner than that. It's the only way to be sure the test results are reliable.

#4: Giving up after your first test fails.

Let's say you had a hypothesis, you tested it, and you were wrong. What now? Well, you still have a problem to solve, which means that you need to change your angle, come up with a new hypothesis, and run another test. Never be discouraged simply because your first test failed.

#5: Running an A/B test with an insufficient amount of traffic.

A/B testing requires traffic. You need to aim for at least 100 conversions per variation, although ideally, you'd wait until you had at least 250 conversions (that's *conversions,* not visitors!). Otherwise, your sample size is too small, and small sample sizes produce unreliable results.

But what should you do if your traffic is much lower than that? Averaging one or two conversions a day means that it will take a long time for you to reach 95% statistical significance. Don't worry – I'll tell you how to deal with that in a minute.

Those are the most common mistakes that people who are new to A/B testing make, and now you know how to avoid them.

Test Everything!

The most important thing to remember as you start A/B testing is that, if you want to increase your conversion rate, you need to test everything. You might have spent a lot of time and energy setting up your landing page, but if your conversions aren't where you want them to be, you have a problem. The good news is that, although it will take some time to do properly, A/B testing can help. Break down each page you want to test into its component parts. It's best to do this in combination with Google Analytics. Pay attention to things like bounce rates and abandoned shopping carts, and use that data to formulate your hypotheses for testing.

What If You Don't Have Enough Traffic?

What do you do if your website doesn't attract enough traffic for running A/B tests? The lower the traffic, the longer it takes to reach statistical significance, and you probably don't have time to run a single test for months until it reaches 95% statistical significance.

If that's the situation you're in, the only way to do conversion rate optimization is to accept that things are going to be messy, and start making educated guesses based on the patterns that you see. For example:

- **Take a look at the data you've gathered.** What are the things that stand out? Do people find a particular feature of your website confusing? Are there problems that come up over and over again? Do the majority of your customers mention the same reason for buying your product? Look for clear patterns.

- **Come up with a hypothesis based on those patterns.** Create a hypothesis that is based on one of those clear patterns.

- **Make the change and see what happens.** Yes, I know I've told you always to test your hypotheses, but this is an exception because you simply don't have the resources to do A/B testing.

Remember when I said that conversion rate optimization was a science? Well, when you don't have enough traffic for A/B testing, the best way to increase your conversion rate is to give something new a try and see what happens. Yes, it's messy, but if you form solid hypotheses that are based on data, you can still increase your conversion rate this way.

Wrapping Things Up

As you can see, conversion rate optimization is a science, and it has a lot of moving parts. If you're new to it, it can seem overwhelming. The key is to take it one step at a time. Familiarize yourself with the basic psychological principles outlined in this chapter, and then think about ways to use them on your website. For example, if you're currently offering customers ten different pricing options, you might use a combination of the paradox of choice and the anchoring effect. You could eliminate several of your pricing options, and use a particular choice as an anchor, thereby steering potential customers toward the option that's the most profitable for you.

When you're coming up with hypotheses to test, don't overlook any aspect of your page. Everything can and should be tested. You can look at:

- Colors
- Fonts
- Text
- Forms
- Incentives
- Layout

Anything that's on any one of your pages can be split-tested to improve conversions. Remember, each page on your site should be optimized for one specific goal. Don't get distracted or try to do too much. Simplicity is the key.

Key Takeaways

Every aspect of your online marketing strategy should be geared toward optimizing your conversion rates.

Conversion rate optimization is all about economics. With digital marketing, you only have two ways to increase sales: you can either attract more traffic to your site, or you can do what you can to convert more traffic. When you do it correctly, conversion rate optimization can help you increase your sales without spending more money.

Conversion rate optimization is a science, and that means you can't skimp on the research if you want results you can rely on. Testing is an essential part of CRO.

Remember that the psychology of conversion rate optimization has three major components: the psychology of influence, which relates to the cognitive biases that influence decision-making processes; the psychology of audience, which relates to having a deep understanding of who your customers are and creating customer personas; and the psychology of design, content and marketing, which relates to individual aspects of your website such as colors, fonts, layout, and headlines.

The six principles of persuasion are the key to optimizing conversions. They are:

- *Reciprocity – giving away something for nothing creates a sense of obligation in your customers.*

- *Commitment and consistency – customers want to be consistent in their actions, so getting them to opt in once makes it easier for them to opt in a second time.*

- *Social proof – customers rely on testimonials and reviews to make decisions, so featuring them on your landing page makes sense.*

- *Authority – people have a tendency to believe what authority figures say, so getting an endorsement from a powerful figure in your industry can be a huge help in terms of overcoming doubts and fears.*

- *Scarcity – most people don't like the feeling that they're missing out on a deal or opportunity. Telling them that the offer is only available for a limited time can help convince them to take action.*

- *Liking – people like people who are attractive and similar to them. They are also susceptible to flattery and compliments, so congratulating them on making a smart decision can be a good move on your part.*

Remember the paradox of choice. More choices are not always better, and presenting too many choices may actually lead to paralysis.

Gathering data is essential. It's best to use a variety of resources, including customer surveys, web analytics and usability testing to help develop hypotheses.

Once you have a hypothesis about something that will increase your conversions, make sure to test it until you have achieved 95% statistical probability. Your test should run for a long enough amount of time to account for differences in web activity based on days of the week.

Test only one element of your sales funnel at a time.

Don't give up if your first hypothesis fails. Come up with a new one and start the process of A/B testing again.

CHAPTER 3

THE PSYCHOLOGY OF WEB DESIGN

Having a well-designed website is important for every business. Potential customers are very likely to check out the website of any company whose product or service they are considering, and a poorly-designed site can scare customers away before they make a purchase. Of course, web design is not as simple as making something that looks nice. Every single element of your website, from the layout to the colors to the fonts, has a psychological impact on your potential customers – and making the right web design choices can mean the difference between success and failure.

Why is web design important for business owners?

First impressions matter. It doesn't matter how great your product or service is – if people don't like the design of your website, they are not going to trust you, and will most likely leave immediately. That might sound harsh, but it's the reality.

Elizabeth Sillence and her team conducted a study on that in 2007. They asked the participants to find websites about hypertension and record whether they trusted or distrusted the website and why. And what was the most common reason for mistrust? A staggering 94% of people cited design problems as being the main issue.[29]

Think about what that means to your business. If the design of your website isn't taking customer psychology into account, you might be losing money because of it. Given how important it is to attract new customers, is that a chance you want to take?

Design has a drastic effect on the conversion rate of a website. You already know how important it is to optimize your site to increase conversions. If the design of your site is contradicting the work you've done to test your conversion pages, all the time you spent split-testing your hypotheses will have been wasted. If you've been thinking that the design of your site isn't that important, think again.

What role does psychology play in web design?

Imagine that you are considering doing business with someone. You schedule a meeting, and they show up in dirty sweatpants and a stained T-shirt, with breadcrumbs all over their clothes, and hair that looks like it hasn't been washed for a week. Would you still want to do business with that person? The answer is probably "No," but do you know why?

The way something is presented affects how we perceive it. So, although that person is the exact same individual whether they look disheveled or sharp, the way they look is going to trigger certain associations in your mind. Those associations will either make it easier or harder for them to persuade you to comply with their requests. So it makes sense for them to make an effort to look appropriate for a business meeting, right?

That's exactly how it works with web design. It doesn't matter how great your content is. If the font is so tiny that it's impossible to read, or if your color scheme makes people dizzy or your design looks amateurish, people are not going to take you seriously.

How can you determine the best design for your website, the one that's going to reassure customers of your trustworthiness and get them to take out their credit cards? That's where psychology comes in. Every aspect of web design has been studied by psychologists. If you want to know the best layout, colors and fonts to use on your website, there is information available to help you do that. The solutions are already there, you just have to apply them.

Design is not about what's pretty, it's about what converts

It's important to understand that when you are running a business, design isn't about having a pretty website; it's about having one that converts. You know those annoying pop-ups that ask you to subscribe to a newsletter? I have never met a single person who likes those things. Everyone hates them. Yet website owners keep using them. Why? It's because those annoying pop-ups work. And that's how you should approach everything in web design. Yes, aesthetics matter, but when you are faced with a design decision, the most important question to ask is "What converts best?"

DESIGN HIERARCHY OF NEEDS

In 1943, an American psychologist named Abraham Maslow proposed the idea that there's a hierarchy to human needs.[30] Take a look at what is often called Maslow's pyramid:

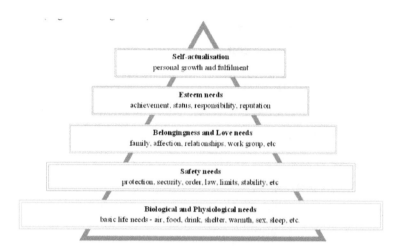

- Physiological needs are about survival. They include air, food, water, clothes, shelter, and sleep. Interestingly enough, Maslow also included sex in this category, although it's not necessary for survival.

- Safety needs are about feeling safe. They include health, personal security, personal stability, being protected by the law, etc.

- Love and belonging needs are about social interactions. They include friendship, intimacy, love, family, community, etc.

- Esteem needs are about self-esteem and recognition from others. They include achievement, prestige, status, recognition, mastery, independence, etc.

- Self-actualization needs are about becoming a better or more complete person. They include peace, knowledge, personal growth, peak experiences, realization of personal potential, etc.

Maslow argued that the needs on the lower levels of the pyramid must be met before higher needs can be pursued. For example, someone who's starving won't care about safety, relationships, recognition, or self-actualization until they satiate their hunger, because survival takes priority over everything else.

Although Maslow's hierarchy of needs intuitively feels right, the idea is often criticized, mainly because it completely ignores a lot of common behavioral patterns. For example, it doesn't account for the behavior of people who are almost entirely focused on self-realization, such as starving artists, monks and nuns, or those who retreat from society altogether, like Tibetan yogis who seek solitude in the mountains. However, there's no such thing as a "one size fits all" solution to any science, including psychology.

Maslow's hierarchy of needs provides a framework for acknowledging and meeting one's needs. It's a great starting place for those who want to build a fulfilling life for themselves. But you might be wondering, what on Earth does this all have to do with web design?

In his essay "Design Hierarchy of Needs" that was published in Smashing Magazine's "Psychology of Web Design" book, web designer Steven Bradley argues that Maslow's hierarchy of needs can be translated to web design.[31] How?

The idea of a design hierarchy of needs is based on the assumption that, in order to be successful, a design must meet basic needs before it can satisfy more sophisticated ones. Bradley's proposed hierarchy goes from functionality, to reliability, to usability, to proficiency, and, finally, to creativity.

Let's take a look at Bradley's pyramid, starting at the bottom:

- Functionality. Your customers need to be able to use your website. For example, if you have an e-commerce store, they need to be able to find and buy products they are interested in. None of your other design elements will matter if your website isn't functional.

- Reliability. Once your website is functioning, it's time to make sure that it's also reliable. For example, if your e-commerce store is often down because of server problems, your customers will go to your competitors' sites instead. Performance of a website needs to be consistent.

- Usability. Your website is functional and reliable, but is it easy to use? Internet users are an impatient bunch, and if they can't immediately figure out how to use your website, they'll move on to something else. If people have stop and figure out how to add products to their shopping cart on your site, chances are they won't be amused. Make sure that your website doesn't come across as a puzzle.

- Proficiency. Only when your website is functioning, reliable, and easy to use should you start to think about adding additional features. For example, having a "Recommended for You" feature on your e-commerce store isn't essential, but it's desirable because it makes it easier for the customer to find products they might be interested in purchasing.

- **Creativity.** Once all the other design needs have been met, you can unleash your creativity. Making your design aesthetically appealing and adding innovative features will help your website stand out.

The design hierarchy of needs provides a framework for thinking about web design the same way Maslow's hierarchy of needs provides a framework for thinking about one's life. It's not perfect, but it's a great starting place.

Layout

The layout of a website is the foundation that you build the rest of your site on. It's important to get it right, because if your foundation is wobbly, aesthetic details aren't going to matter. So what should you keep in mind when conceptualizing the layout of your website?

F-shaped pattern

Nielsen Norman Group, a company that specializes in user experience, conducted an eye-tracking study in 2006 in which they recorded the way 232 users looked at thousands of web pages. They found that the reading pattern remained fairly consistent no matter what type of website the users were looking at.[32]

According to Jakob Nielsen, the dominant reading pattern looks somewhat like the letter F, and has three main components:

- Users start reading with a horizontal movement, usually across the upper part of the content area, which forms the top bar of the F.

- Next, they move down the page a bit, and do a second horizontal movement, which is typically shorter than the first one, forming the lower bar of the F.

- Finally, they scan the website's left side in a vertical movement, and this forms the stem of the F.

Users don't follow a precise F pattern 100% of the time, but generally, reading patterns resemble the letter F. The main variable from one site to the next was the distance between the top bar and the lower bar. Here are some examples to show you the variations on the pattern.

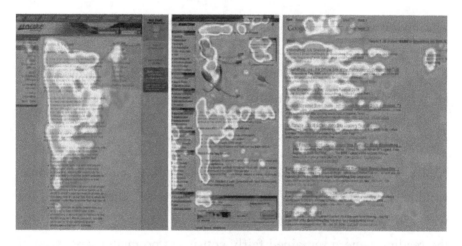

It's important to keep this F-shaped pattern in mind. You want to increase your conversion rate? Make sure to place the most important elements of your page in the places where they are most likely to get noticed.

Top left corner

When someone lands on your site, what is the first thing they look at? According to Nielsen, their eye path starts at the upper left corner. What do you want them to see first? When a visitor lands on your website, you must make it clear why your products or services are valuable to them. This means that the upper left corner is the place where you should put your value proposition. That's why companies often put their logo and slogan there.

Top Menu

Once people are done with the logo and slogan, their eyes will make a horizontal move across the page. That's where your main navigation menu should be. Avoid drop-down menus whenever possible. Usability studies by Nielsen Norman Group show that users find them annoying[33] – they perceive it as an unnecessary hurdle. Plus, drop down menus mean that you have less control over the way users move around your web site, and that might lead to them skipping important pages. One other thing to consider is the number of items on your main navigation menu – try to have no more than five, since more choices may end up confusing your customers.

Left Sidebar.

You already know that when a user lands on your website, he starts reading at the top left corner, and then moves in an F-shaped pattern. What that means is that he pays more attention to the left side of the page he's viewing. In fact, another Nielsen study in 2010 showed that web users spend 69% of their time viewing the left half of the page and 30% of their time viewing the right half.[34] That means that you should place the elements that you want people to pay attention to (such as a vertical menu, an opt-in form, or an ad) on the left sidebar.

You should also try to keep text (for example, blog posts) on the left side of the page or at least in the center of the page. Placing it on the right side of the page will decrease the likelihood of it being read. The introductory paragraph of each article or blog post should be more noticeable than the rest of the text. One way to do that is to bold the opening paragraph or put it in italics. It's also a good idea to add a picture to the introductory paragraph.

As for the body of the text, you should make it easy to skim because that's how most people consume online content. That means that the paragraphs should be short, the page should have plenty of white space, and you should use sub-headlines to break up the text.

It also important to know that images can help you enhance the perceived validity of your claims. That was proven by Eryn J. Newman, Maryanne Garry, Daniel M. Bernstein, Justin Kantner, and D. Stephen Lindsay in a series of experiments they conducted in 2012.[35] In experiment 1, the researchers showed the participants familiar and unfamiliar celebrity names, and participants had to rate claims about whether each celebrity was alive or dead as true or false. Some names were shown alone, and some were shown accompanied by a photo of the celebrity in question. Guess what? For unfamiliar celebrities, the photo increased the likelihood that participants would judge the claim to be true, regardless of whether the claim was "alive" or "dead." In other words, the study showed that people tend to perceive statements that are accompanied by photos as more true than ones that are presented in text-only format. You should take that into consideration when trying to decide where to place images in the body of your text.

Using photos, infographics, videos, etc. in the body of your text will help you to break it up and make it more readable and appealing.

Images

Jakob Nielsen from Nielsen Norman Group recommends using large, crisp images in your web design to give your website a professional look.

Image quality is a significant factor when it comes to drawing attention. You want to avoid using images that are small and of a poor quality. Users are not impressed by cheesy stock photos.

The Halo Effect is something to keep in mind when choosing images for your websites. Remember how people tend to perceive attractive men and women as more intelligent, kind and trustworthy? Well, attractive people can cast a "halo" on your products or services, making whatever you sell appear more desirable. A 2008 study showed that men were more likely to take financial risks, such as buying an expensive car, if they saw erotic images of women first.[36] That's the Halo Effect in action, and car manufacturers can take advantage of it by putting attractive women in their ads.

You can probably improve your conversion rates by using pictures of attractive people on your website. However, it's important to make sure that you depict people your audience can relate to. If your customers are moms in their 30s, then using pictures of a high school cheerleader isn't going to help. In fact, Jakob Nielsen says that people who look like models are less likely to draw attention than "normal" people. So if you want to take advantage of the Halo Effect, use pictures of people who belong to the same demographic group as your target audience and would be considered attractive within that group, but who aren't necessarily attractive in the way professional models are.

Keep the most important things above the fold!

In terms of positioning things on your page, it's important to keep the serial position effect in mind to get the maximum impact.

In his 1913 book *Memory: A Contribution to Experimental Psychology*, a German psychologist named Herman Ebbinghaus performed a series of memory experiments on himself. The experiments were later repeated and verified by other people. What Ebbinghaus found is that his recall accuracy varied depending on an item's position within a list.[37] The phenomenon he described is actually a combination of two psychological effects:

- Primacy effect. The primacy effect is a cognitive bias that results in a subject recalling information that's presented earlier in a series or piece of content more accurately that information that's presented later on.

■ Recency effect. The recency effect is a cognitive bias that results in a subject recalling the most recently presented information the best.

It may seem that the primacy and recency effects are in conflict with one another, but when you combine them it simply means that people tend to recall the information that was presented first and the information that was presented last the best, an effect that Ebbinghaus dubbed the serial position effect. But what does this have to do with web design?

You can see the serial position effect in action if you take a look at the habits of Internet users. They don't scroll as much as you think. The part of the website that is above the fold – that is, the part that you see without having to scroll down – gets the lion's share of attention. That means that you need to keep the most important elements of your website – logo, value proposition, email opt-in form, etc. -- above the fold. You can also add these things to the very bottom of your website since users will often scroll to the bottom of a page before navigating away. Things that are in between will be forgotten easily. What's more, they often don't get seen at all since users tend to either not scroll at all or scroll straight to the very bottom.

Okay, so now that you understand how to build the foundation of your website, let's talk about color.

Color Scheme

Colors have a dramatic impact on the way people perceive things – which means that they can have a big impact on your revenue, too.

For example, when Microsoft was designing Bing, they tested a lot of colors and it turned out that a particular shade of blue was what people clicked the most. How big of an impact did the choice of that color have? "That blue was worth at least $80 million," said Paul Ray, Bing's user experience manager at the time.

The lesson there is that it pays to put a lot of thought into your color choices. After all, the way you present your brand is the way people are going to perceive it, so you better be sure that your color scheme is an excellent match for your business. But how?

Here are five factors that you need to pay attention to when it comes to choosing a color scheme for your website:

#1: Appropriateness of color

A 2006 study conducted by Paul Bottomley and John Doyle showed that, when it comes to choosing the colors for your brand, the most important thing is the appropriateness of those colors.[38] For example, they found that functional products were perceived in a more positive way if they were associated with functional colors. Meanwhile, sensory-social products performed best when they were associated with sensory-social colors.

A functional color is one that's associated strongly with a particular industry. For example, there's a reason that John Deere uses green as the primary color of their logo. Their products are used in farming, and the color green is a natural fit for their brand.

Products that are not functional do best when they are associated with colors that convey social status or luxury rather than functionality. A classic example would be Tiffany blue, the color that jewelry giant Tiffany & Co. uses on its boxes and bags. The color they use, similar to robin's egg blue, has nothing to do with jewelry per se.

People associate different colors with different kinds of businesses. It's important to make sure that the color scheme that you use on your website is seen as appropriate for your particular business. Your customers will not be impressed if it appears to be a complete mismatch for whatever it is that you are selling. For example, using pink and green for a funeral home website is probably not a good idea. It's not the individual colors that matter, it's their appropriateness for your business.

#2: Meaning of color

The issue of color appropriateness is more complicated than it might seem at first glance because colors have different meanings in different cultures. For example, in China the color red is associated with good fortune, while in South Africa it's associated with death and mourning. You have to take cultural differences into account if you want your customers to perceive your color scheme as appropriate for your product or service.

Let's look at just one example to get an idea of how the meaning of a color can change across cultures. The color blue can represent:

- Western countries – the male gender, depression, corporate conservatism

- China – Immortality and spirituality

- Iran – Mourning

- Eastern – Wealth and self-cultivation

- Cherokee – Defeat

As you can see, there's a lot of room for interpretation. You don't want to use the color blue to convey masculinity in Iran, or the color red to symbolize sex in China. Understanding the symbolism of colors will help you make your color scheme a better fit for your product or service.

#3: Color preferences by gender

A 2003 study by Joe Hallock[39] looked at differences in color preferences by gender. While the differences weren't dramatic, they are relevant. Blue was the most popular color of both genders, but among women, purple (a color that is not a favorite among men) placed second. Of course, these gender color preferences are largely cultural, and dependent on current trends. For example, did you know that back in the day, light blue was considered feminine and pink was considered masculine? However, it's important to understand the gender color preferences in the culture in which you are operating your business.

A 2007 study by Carol Auster and Claire Mansbach found that there was a clear difference in the colors used in toys meant for boys and girls.[40] Not only that, but toys that were marketed to both boys and girls skewed heavily to colors associated with boys. Their theory is that boys are less likely to cross gender lines than girls are.

It's important to keep the gender of your customers in mind when you are looking for the right color scheme – if the majority of your customers are men, then you should use colors that appeal to men, and vice versa. For example, in the US alone there are millions of women who ride motorcycles. However, there are way more men who do so, so if you are selling motorcycles, then it makes sense not to use purple since that is a color that appeals more to women than to men. That might seem exclusionary, but when you are making big decisions, you have to focus on the preferences of your core customers.

#4: *Von Restorff effect*

As I'm sure you remember, the Von Restorff effect refers to the fact that an item that stands out like a sore thumb is more likely to be remembered than something that blends in with its surroundings, as demonstrated in Hedwig von Restorff's memory experiments.

However, in web design, it's less about getting people to remember something, and more about getting them to click something. You want your call-to-action elements – links, buttons, banners, etc. - to stand out from everything else on your website. One thing that a lot of web designers do is choose a color that's complementary to their main color scheme.

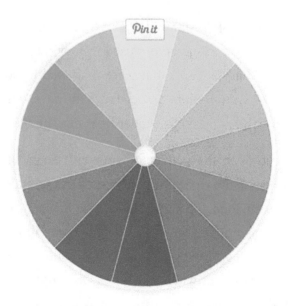

Complementary colors are colors that are opposite one another on a color wheel like the one above. So for example, on a predominantly blue page, gold or orange might make a good choice for the opt-in button. Just remember that what stands out gets clicked.

#5: Active and passive colors

There are several ways to think about color coordination and using the Von Restorff effect in web design. One useful framework is the active colors/passive colors method proposed by online marketing expert Derek Halpern. He advises to have passive colors that you use for everything except call-to-action elements as well as an active color that you use for call-to-action elements only. This way, you train people on when and what to click, and that makes them more likely to respond to your calls to action. Just don't forget the Von Restorff effect – make sure that your action color stands out in your particular color scheme. Here's a great example from WebDAM, which uses the complementary colors blue and orange to make their calls to action stand out.

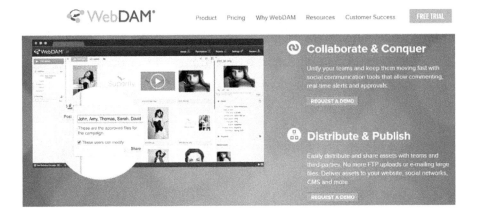

All of the above information shows why choosing the right colors for your website is so important. If you select colors that don't make sense to your customers on an emotional level, you risk alienating them before they even get a chance to evaluate your product or service. There are very few people who would hire financial advisers whose site was mostly red, for example. If your call to action doesn't stand out, people might not notice it. The colors you choose for your website can have a significant impact both on how your customers perceive you, and on your bottom line.

Typography

Typography is the art and technique of arranging type to make written language readable and appealing. It's not something that people normally pay attention to unless they have a design background. However, no company with a web presence can afford to overlook it.

Typography plays a big role in the way your company is perceived. Can you imagine a CEO of a Fortune 500 company using Comic Sans font for a business document? Very few of his clients would be amused if he did such a thing because it flies in the face of their expectations of him. His clients want to see a professional and conservative font. Different fonts trigger different associations, and in order to leave a great first impression you have to make sure that you are using fonts that are right for your business.

Company Folders, an online printing firm, did an in-depth analysis of the psychology of fonts on their blog recently.[41] Here's some of what they revealed:

- Serif. Serif fonts include Baskerville, Bodini, Garamond, Georgia, and Times New Roman. These fonts send a message of authority, tradition, and respect. You should use these fonts if you want your website to appear serious in an old-fashioned, corporate way. Don't use them for anything that is supposed to look fun.

- Sans Serif. Sans Serif fonts include Arial, Calibri, Century Gothic, Helvetica, and Verdana. These fonts are clean and modern, and they send a message that you are objective, stable, and universal. Sans serif fonts make a good choice for almost any website because they are more legible than serif fonts when read on a computer.

- Slab Serif. Slab Serif fonts include Bevan, Clarendon, Courier, Museo, and Rockwell. These fonts tend to be bold and strong, and they send the message that the company who uses them is modern, solid, and funky. These fonts are great for businesses that want to convey a fun and youthful vibe. However, they can be a bit much when used in the main body of your text. Use them sparingly.

- Script Serif. Script Serif fonts include Brush Script, Lobster, Lucida, Pacifico, and Zapfino. These fonts are elegant and feminine, and they let customers know that your company is creative, friendly, and intriguing. They work well for logos for businesses in creative industries, or companies whose target customers are primarily women. They make a poor choice for anything other than a logo or site name. As a rule, they are too busy to be used for subheadings or the body of your text, or for anything conservative or corporate.

■ Modern. Modern fonts include Infinity, Eurostyle, Majoram, Matchbook, and Politica. These fonts are sharp and stylish, and they send the message that your company is exclusive, fashionable, and intelligent. They work well in headers and logos for hip businesses whose core customers are young. Don't use them for anything old-fashioned or corporate.

Another thing that is important to keep in mind is the size of the font you use on your website. Reading on a screen is not the same as reading a printed text. A 12-point font might be perfect for a paperback book, but when text that size is displayed on the screen, it's hard on the eyes. Nobody wants to strain their eyes in order to read a blog post. They're far more likely to leave, and that's not what you want.

It's a good rule of thumb to think of a 14-point font as the minimum in terms of size, but you may be better served by using fonts larger than that. For example, the HelpScout blog uses a 26-point font for their introductory paragraph and a 19-point font for the rest of the post, like this:

I f email support is your core responsibility, then writing to communicate well is your art, and a professional must take his or her art seriously.

In the same way an architect must be adept with his hands and have a love for mathematics, those who do customer support must exercise empathy and communicate it through writing.

As Mark Twain memorably said:

> *"The difference between the right word and the almost right word is the difference between lightning and a lightning bug."*

Printed text that size would look like something that belongs in the children's section of a bookstore, but when displayed on a computer screen, the text is easy to read. There's no need to drive people away by using small fonts when you can use large fonts that make for a much more pleasant reading experience.

When you choose a font that matches up with the image that you want to project to your customers, you offer them a subtle reassurance that you can deliver on your promises. Make sure that you use fonts that convey the message that you want to convey – and that are large enough to be read on the screen.

Directional Cues

Directional cues are visual elements that nudge visitors towards taking the action that you want them to take. There are two types of directional cues:

- Explicit cues. Explicit cues are the visual sign posts that guide the user towards something that you want them to see (e.g. arrows, lines, etc.)

- Suggestive cues. Suggestive cues are more subtle than explicit cues. They use imagery to guide the user (e.g. a picture of a person looking at your call to action button, etc.).

Directional cues might seem cheesy, especially the explicit cues such as arrows. The reason they are employed so frequently, cheesy or not, is because they work.

Giovanni Galfano and his team ran an interesting experiment in 2012.[42] He told the participants to look out for a small target that would appear on a screen and press the spacebar as soon as they saw it. That target would appear either on the left-hand side or the right-hand side of the page. The researchers made things easier for the participants to follow by having a directional word, either "Left" or "Right", appear on the screen immediately before the target appeared.

They also threw in something designed to confound the participants. After the directional word appeared, a directional cue in the form of a cartoon face or an arrow would appear. It could be pointing in either direction -- the cartoon character would be "pointing" by looking left or right. The study subjects were told to ignore the directional cues and focus only on the target, aided by the directional words.

What the study showed was that every time the arrow or face was pointing in the wrong direction, it took the subjects a few milliseconds longer to press the space bar. A few milliseconds might not seem like much, but it is statistically significant.

There are a lot of different ways to use directional cues. You could go with a straightforward arrow pointing people to your opt-in form, or you could try something a bit more whimsical, like this example from project management company Basecamp:

Chaos, organized.

Basecamp keeps people on same page so no matter what your role is, everyone works toward a common goal: **finishing a project** *together.*

Their page is very effective because it makes use of multiple lines to let customers know at a glance that their product is designed to bring all the different parts of a project together.

Regardless of how you decide to implement them, people have a very hard time resisting directional cues. If you use them wisely, you'll increase your conversion rates.

7 Most Common Design Mistakes

Now that you understand the basic components of effective web design and how you can use them to influence your customers, let's stop a moment to look at the most common design mistakes companies make and how you can avoid them.

#1: Cluttered layout

There are a lot of bells and whistles out there available for you to use on your website. When you start designing, you might be tempted to add every widget and plugin you can find, along with social media share and follow buttons and advertising. Resist the temptation. Most internet users don't like cluttered layouts. Too much information on the page can overwhelm your customers. When you have too many design elements on your page, the things that really matter – like your message and your call to action – can get lost in the shuffle. When that happens, your conversion rates can plummet, and that's not what you want.

The solution is to stick to clean and simple designs. A page with plenty of white space, beautiful and relevant images, easily readable content, appropriate fonts and colors, and intuitive navigation is a pleasure for customers to visit. Any time you're tempted to add a new design element to your website, stop a minute to ask yourself whether you *really* need it. If it doesn't serve a purpose, it's just a distraction.

#2: Confusing navigation

Anybody who's ever surfed the internet has encountered a difficult-to-navigate website. You know what I'm talking about. You land on the page and start looking for a search box or menu, but those things are nowhere to be found. Maybe the menu is there, but it's in an unconventional place like the bottom of the page. Other confusing navigational elements include counter-intuitive designs, links that aren't highlighted, or a search option that's hidden. When you run across confusing navigation, what do you do? Do you think, "Wow, this is amazing, this website is so innovative!"? Of course not. You probably react the same way most people would. You might click around for a few seconds looking for what you need, and then you would become annoyed and click on the back button to find a site that was easier to use.

Your visitors shouldn't have to spend their valuable time trying to figure out how your website works. Most websites use the same standard navigation template, meaning that they have:

- A main menu that's always visible and in a conventional place (at the top of the page or along the left side)

- Two of three tiers of pages that are easy to understand

- Links that are highlighted in a way that makes them easy to see and identify

- A search option that's easy to find, usually at the top right-hand side of the page

Your site should do the same. For example, if you have an e-commerce store, then it should be similar to other e-commerce stores, because that's what your customers expect. Don't try to reinvent the wheel.

When it comes to navigation, your website should be similar to other websites of the same type, otherwise people will be confused and irritated, and your conversion rate will be low.

#3: Low contrast fonts.

Do you know why black text on a white background is so easy to read? It's because of the contrast between the background color and the font.

If you use a light font on a light background or a dark font on a dark background, you can be pretty sure that nobody is going to read your content. Reading something that's in low contrast puts a strain on your customers' eyes. Reading on a computer can be problematic anyway, and you don't want to give people a reason to navigate away from your page.

Always use high contrast fonts – either a dark background with a light font, or a light background with a dark font. Just keep in mind that it's important to choose the right colors too. You remember how they used bright green text on a black background in the movie "The Matrix"? That type of thing looks great on film, but it would render your text completely unreadable on a computer screen. Pick high contrast colors that are appropriate for your company.

#4: Fonts that are too small.

There was a time when most websites had small fonts. In fact, the standard font size was 12 points, the same font size that is used in most printed texts. Those were the early days of the internet, before we started studying how people read internet pages, and things have changed.

Ask yourself a question: "Am I using at least a 14-point font for the body of my text?" If the answer is "No" you should enlarge your fonts immediately. If it's "Yes" you should still take a look at the readability of your page. 14 points is the minimum, but you might want to consider going to 16 or 18 points.

#5: Big blocks of text

Another common mistake people make is having big blocks of text on their page. White space is important. Enormous paragraphs might be okay for a philosophy treatise, but they're not okay for the internet. If your blog posts are walls of text, you can be pretty sure that no one is going to read them. What should you do instead?

Most people don't read online content, they skim it – and you should accommodate that tendency. Break your text up with sub headlines and images, keep the paragraphs at a maximum of three or four lines, and make sure that there's plenty of white space between the paragraphs. This will make your content more appealing to users and will increase the chances of it being read.

#6: Too many calls to action

Remember the paradox of choice? The more options you offer, the more overwhelmed people feel, and the more likely they are to simply do nothing. This also applies to design.

The more cluttered your design, the more likely people are to become paralyzed by it. If you bombard your users with calls to action, they might not know what to look at first. When you try to do too much at once, it can have a negative effect on your conversion rates.

Each page on your website should have one goal, and it should be optimized for that one goal. For example, if your priority is building an email list, then make sure you have an easy-to-see opt-in box. If you have a very long page of content, it might make sense to put the same call to action at various points on the page to make it convenient for people to fill out your form. You can conduct tests to determine if you need to repeat your call to action on the page. The main thing to remember is not to ask people to subscribe to your list, schedule a free consultation and buy your product all on the same page. That's a sure way to induce a paradox of choice.

#7: *Outdated look.*

The Internet is an extremely fast-paced environment. That means that your web design, no matter how great it looks now, is going to age quickly. 2012 might seem like it was just yesterday – and it was, in human years. But in internet years that's ages ago, which means that designs that looked great in 2012 seem outdated in 2015. Having an outdated website in an age of progress and innovation is *not* going to do your business any good. I'm not saying that you should do a web design make-over every week, but if it's been a couple of years since you've revamped your design, you should think about updating it to keep up with the current trends.

These seven mistakes are not the only things that can go wrong with your website, but they are some of the most common web design mistakes businesses make.

Wrapping Things Up

The most important thing to remember about web design is that every single element of your website, from the fonts to the layout, makes a difference when it comes to conversion. If just one element is off, it can make potential customers navigate away from your page.

That might seem overwhelming to think about, but the information in this chapter can help you make the right choices. As long as you take care to pick colors that are appropriate for your industry and product, a font that reinforces the attributes that customers are looking for, and a layout that is intuitive and easy to navigate, then your design will do everything it is supposed to do.

Key Takeaways

Design problems can lead customers to mistrust your website.

Psychology affects every aspect of web design, including the layout of your pages and the colors and fonts you choose.

The primary job of web design is to get customers to convert.

Remember the design hierarchy of needs:

- *Functionality first – does your website work?*

- *Reliability – is it available when people need it?*

- *Usability – is it easy to use and navigate?*

- *Proficiency – what extra features can you add to make the experience more valuable to users?*

■ *Creativity – is your website aesthetically pleasing?*

■ *People read web pages in a particular (and predictable) way. Some of the key things to remember are:*

■ *People read in an "F" pattern starting on the left side of the page.*

■ *Web users spend nearly twice as much time on the left margin of the page than they do anywhere else.*

■ *People skim before reading, so white space is very important. Use subheadings, frequent paragraph breaks and bullet points to break up big blocks of text.*

■ *People respond well to images when they break up the text.*

Remember the Halo Effect and use quality images of attractive people that your customer can identify with.

Primacy and recency indicate that customers tend to pay the most attention to content that's above the fold (before they have to scroll down) and at the bottom of the page. Remember what we said early on about the old brain remembering what's at the beginning and end of your presentation, and apply it to your web design.

Color choices can have a huge impact on how people react to your page. Remember the main aspects of color selection:

- *Appropriateness (use functional colors for functional products)*

- *Meaning (colors mean different things in different cultures)*

- *Gender preferences and associations*

- *Von Restorff Effect (people notice colors that stick out)*

Typography can send a strong message about your company and what it does. Readability should always be your first concern, but after that make sure that you choose a font that's congruent with your brand and product.

Directional cues can help visitors to your site know what to do next.

Avoid the most common design mistakes: cluttered layout, confusing navigation, low-contrast fonts, fonts that are too small, big blocks of text, too many calls to action, and outdated design.

CHAPTER 4

PERSUASIVE WRITING FUNDAMENTALS

"Persuasion is often more effectual than force."
~ Aesop

Any writing that you do on behalf of your business is persuasive writing by nature. It doesn't matter whether you are coming up with the title of a blog post, sending an email to your client list, or posting content on social media. Its goal, ultimately, is to convince the people who read it to take some kind of action.

Some of the writing you do may be intended to convince people who see your AdWords ad to click on the ad and visit your website. When a potential client visits your website, the writing that appears there is intended to get them to call you and set up an appointment. Writing on your blog or on social media may be aimed at building your reputation or providing your clients with valuable information. Regardless of what the specific goal is, the general goal is persuasion.

People use persuasion all the time. When a politician gives a speech or when you see a commercial on television, the words that you hear are persuasive. The politician wants you to vote for her instead of the other candidates. The company that paid for the commercial wants to convince you to buy their product instead of their competitor's. It's not a complicated thing. However, as you might expect, it is a scientific thing.

The human brain is vulnerable to persuasion, but to write persuasively you need to understand the things that will help you get around the brain's defense mechanisms. I'm talking about cognitive biases and rationalizations – all the things that tell your potential clients that they shouldn't hire your firm or buy your product.

Many of the things we've discussed previously apply to persuasive writing, too. However, in this chapter we'll focus exclusively on persuasive writing. The psychology of persuasive writing is such that you can apply it to any digital content, whether it's on your website, your emails, or on social media. One of the great things about writing online is that what you write can be almost any length, which gives you the opportunity to address all of a potential client's objections and persuade them to hire you.

Before we start talking specifics, let's take a minute to discuss why knowing how to write persuasively is essential for anyone writing digital content. Good writing is the same whether it appears in a newspaper, magazine, web site, letter, or is written on a napkin. There's a misconception that the medium changes the message, and that the Internet has irreversibly altered consumers' buying habits. That's all nonsense, of course, and should be ignored. While there are medium-specific considerations to take into account, good persuasive content is the lynchpin of almost every marketing strategy. Learn to write it well, and you will be rewarded in kind.

Keys to Good Persuasive Writing

Before we start breaking down persuasive writing in a more detailed way, let's talk about a few fundamentals. Here are some basic things to keep in mind:

- Sell the customer benefits (what problem the product can solve for them) instead of a list of features.

- Keep yourself out of the way (remember that the archaic mind only cares about itself)

- Use easy to understand language written in a conversational manner.

If you study some of the most successful writers online, you'll note that they always adhere to these three basic principles.

Now let's talk about some specifics.

The Psychology of Headlines.

The first thing people will see, regardless of where your content appears, is your headline. Don't let the word "headline" put you off – a headline could be the title of your web page or of a blog post, the subject of an email, or the title of anything you post on social media. Whatever the format, you can expect that about 60% of the people who encounter it will read only the headline according to a study by the American Press Institute.[46] Because your headline represents your best chance to convince a potential client to keep reading, you need to make sure it's as effective as possible. How do you do this? Let's start by talking about the goal of a headline.

The Goal of a Headline

The goal of a headline (or a blog title or email subject line) is to persuade the people who see it to take the next step, whether it's opening the email, reading your blog post, or picking up the phone to schedule an appointment. The goal of a headline may vary depending upon where it appears, but ultimately, the intention is to convince potential clients that they can trust you and should hire you.

In his book *Advertising Headlines that Make You Rich*, David Garfinkel breaks down some of the most successful headlines of all time into basic templates that can be adapted to almost any format or industry. Let's look at some examples before we talk about specific psychological principles that you can use to craft persuasive headlines.

If You're Out of the Market Now, You'll Hate Yourself Later[47]

This headline was originally written by Don Hauptman for an investment newsletter. The reason that it's so effective is that it plays on a natural fear people have – the fear of losing out. Garfinkel points out that this headline can be used for many different situations. For example, a law firm that specializes in helping entrepreneurs incorporate their businesses might say, "If You Don't Incorporate Now, You'll Hate Yourself Later."

The reason that this headline is effective is because it will make the people who see it ask questions: Why will I hate myself later? What are the benefits of incorporation? It's simple and powerful.

Here's one more example before we move on:

Now You Can Create a Breakthrough Marketing Plan Within the Next 30 Days...for FREE[48]

Why it works: This headline presents a clear time frame, and it's short, offering tremendous benefits in a brief period. Hyperbolic discounting – a cognitive bias that makes people more likely to accept immediate rewards over long-term gains -- encourages us to learn more about this, as we envision how different our lives can be in just 30 days if we craft an amazing new marketing plan.[49]

Offering something for free is one of the best ways of overcoming a client's objections and fears. The word "Free" makes a transaction frictionless. It can be adapted to any business – a lot of service companies offer a free consultation or something of that nature to get people to pick up the phone and schedule an appointment.

Free is far, far more powerful than "cheap." Dan Ariely demonstrated this with a study that offered participants their choice of chocolate: either a Hershey's kiss or a Lindt chocolate truffle.[50] They were originally offered for sale at the nominal prices of one cent and 15 cents, respectively. The Lindt truffle was offered for less than its actual cost.

About 75% of the study's participants purchased the truffle. That makes sense -- it was a premium product being offered for a discount, and was a superior offering to the Kiss.

Then the researchers made the Kiss free, and the Lindt truffle 14 cents. In other words, they reduced the price by just one cent on each item. That shouldn't make much of a difference, right? One cent is practically nothing and has no value on its own.

The preference, however, quickly reversed itself. Over 67% of participants chose the free Kiss in lieu of the truffle, which was still being offered for a deep discount.

How does this apply to your digital marketing efforts? Even if you're not offering a tangible product for sale, you can adapt the principle of "free" to what you do offer. I already mentioned that many service companies, such as accountants and lawyers, offer potential clients a free initial consultation to get them in the door. However, there are other ways to use the word "free" to win over readers. For example, you might combine it with other words to say that your services are risk-free. Remember, overcoming a prospect's aversion to risk is one of the most important goals of persuasive writing.

Now that we've examined some effective headlines, let's talk about specific psychological principles that apply to headline writing and how you can use them to get people to click your ads, open your emails, and read your content.

Headline Techniques to Use

Regardless of your business or industry, there are certain psychological techniques you can use to write headlines that capture a reader's attention. Note: I am using the word "headline" but these techniques could apply to titles of articles or blog posts and email subject lines as well. This section will look at six such techniques, explaining the science behind them and how you can use them for your own persuasive writing.

Surprise

Surprising someone with a headline is one of the best ways to get them to keep reading. In their book *Made to Stick: Why Some Ideas Survive and Others Die*, Chip and Dan Heath talk about how their research indicates that people are attuned to the expected.[51] The use of surprise breaks the pattern of what's expected and arouses our interest. In other words, surprise captures a reader's attention and interest holds it.

Part of the reason why surprise is such an effective headline-writing technique is that it activates the pleasure centers of our brains. It turns out that we react more intensely to pleasure that we don't expect than to pleasure that we do, as was demonstrated in a study conducted by Gregory Berns of Emory and Read Montague of Baylor.[52] Their research examined participants' reactions to having water or fruit juice squirted into their mouths at unpredictable intervals. For participants who preferred the fruit juice, the pleasure of receiving it unexpectedly was higher than it was when they simply drank the juice.

How does this apply to your digital marketing efforts? The chances are that there's a way to present your business or services in a way that would surprise people. It could be as simple as using an unexpected word in the subject line of an email, the way Barack Obama did. One of the emails he sent to his supporters had this subject line: "Hell yeah, I like Obamacare." The unexpected insertion of the word "Hell" created surprise and garnered a very high response.

I'm not suggesting you should use profanity in your digital marketing campaigns, but think about ways to tweak your vocabulary and offer something unexpected. Let's look at an example from a law firm's blog:

Ex-husband allegedly used Wite-Out to avoid alimony payments

This headline works because it's surprising. It's not a question of surprise vocabulary as much as it is the suggestion of a surprising action. It's hard not to be both surprised and curious when reading that headline, which means that it's done its job.

Negatives

A 2013 study by the content marketers at Outbrain looked at 65,000 headlines to discover which ones did the best job of engaging readers' interest. What they found is that negative superlatives (words like *worst* and *least*) got far more attention than positive words.[53] In fact, headlines that used positive superlatives performed 29% worse than headlines with no superlatives, and headlines with negative superlatives performed 30% better than those with no superlatives. That means that negative superlatives performed 63% better than positive ones – a remarkable difference.

Why are negative headlines so effective? It may be due in part to a natural tendency to doubt the motivation behind positive superlatives – call it cynicism. But it's more likely because our brains process negative information differently than they do positive information. A 1998 study in the Journal of Personality and Social Psychology[54] demonstrated a profound negativity bias in the human brain. What that means is that we give a lot of importance to negative information, so negative headlines have a bigger impact than positive ones do.

The preference for negative headlines may be linked to the survival instinct as well. Remember that the reptilian brain always has to be satisfied first. Negative headlines and words may trigger the fight-or-flight response, making it harder for us to ignore them.

How can the negativity bias help you with your digital marketing efforts? If you have a blog, you may want to find a way to include intriguing negatives in your blog titles – and the same goes for the subject lines of emails. You can even take a positive and flip it around, saying something like, "10 Mistakes to Avoid if You Want Your Firm to be Profitable." You get the idea.

Numbers

What is it about numbers? A Conductor study in 2013 showed that headlines that featured numbers were more popular than any other kind of headline.[55] Not only that, it found that the higher the number was, the more likely people were to select the headline in question.

One reason may be due to a cognitive bias known as the *Numerosity Heuristic*. It turns out that when it comes to numbers and the way we perceive them, bigger really is better. We attach more importance and value to high numbers than we do to low ones.[56]

How does this apply to your digital marketing efforts? Well, everyone who writes persuasive headlines could take a lesson from the viral content whizzes at Buzzfeed. A look at their home page shows that most of the articles featured have a number in the headline. To translate the strategy for your business, try incorporating numbers into your email marketing or blog posts. Let's try a different take on the earlier example I gave you:

If You Don't Incorporate Now, You'll Hate Yourself Later

If you wanted to put a number in this headline, you could try something like:

14 Reasons to Incorporate Right Now

A headline like that arouses the interest of unincorporated entrepreneurs. Hint: using an unusual number can add an element of surprise, too. Top ten lists are fairly common. Fourteen reasons? That's unexpected.

The Curiosity Gap

The next psychological principle that can help you write persuasive headlines is the *Curiosity Gap*, a term that was coined by Carnegie Mellon professor George Loewenstein to describe the gap between what we know and what we would like to know.[57] You might have heard that curiosity killed the cat, but when it comes to writing headlines that will get people to read your content, curiosity may just be your saving grace.

How does it work? First of all, it's impossible for a person to be curious about a topic that's completely unfamiliar. A headline that uses curiosity effectively will offer an intriguing piece of information that arouses curiosity without satisfying it. Second, it turns out that curiosity actually makes us anticipate pleasure. According to a CalTech study that asked participants trivia questions and measured the way their brains responded, curiosity increases activity in the caudate area of the brain, which is linked to anticipation of rewards.[58]

To put the curiosity gap to work for you, try to pick an intriguing fact from your web page or email, and put part of it in your title or subject line. Look at this example from Upworthy:

What happens when an artist's hand starts to shake is a lesson for us all.

This is a classic example of the Curiosity Gap in action. It makes readers curious: What happens? What's the lesson for me? There are plenty of ways to incorporate curiosity into a headline about any topic. Just take the most interesting information from your article or blog post and tease it in the headline.

Specificity

The same Conductor study we discussed earlier also found that readers have a high preference for headlines that let them know exactly what to expect from an email or article. That might seem to contradict what I just said about curiosity, but it's actually a byproduct of media saturation. When people are bombarded with content, as they are any time they're online, it's natural to want to know that their expectations of an article will be met when they click on it.

Why do people prefer specificity over vagueness? One reason may be that we have a natural prejudice against uncertainty, a phenomenon known as the *Ambiguity Effect*.[59] First identified by Daniel Ellsberg in 1961, the Ambiguity Effect shows that people are inclined to choose situations where the probability of a particular result is known over those where the probability is unknown.

On the surface, that might not appear to have anything to do with persuasive writing, but the marketing takeaway is that sometimes letting your readers know exactly what to expect is a good idea. Let's look at another example from Upworthy:

3 moms had no way to fly to see their hero sons honored. So a CEO lent them his private jet.

For him, it was a small gesture. For them, it meant everything.

A reader who sees this headline knows exactly what she's going to get if she clicks on it – a heartwarming story about a businessman using his wealth to help someone deserving. There's no ambiguity – only a promise that's fulfilled by reading the article in question.

How can you use specificity in your digital marketing? Find a clear but interesting way to convey what people will learn if they read your article. Look at this example from business blog Bufferapp:

Readers know from reading the headline that the article is about the ideal length of online content, and that it's not just someone's recommendations – it's backed by science.

Referencing the Audience

The final principle we'll discuss in relation to headline writing is referencing the audience. A 2014 study from Norway found that headlines that referenced the audience directly got higher click-through rates than headlines that were purely informational.[60] The three examples they used were:

For Sale: Black iPhone4 16GB

Anyone Need a New iPhone4?

Is This Your New iPhone4?

The third option – the one that references the audience directly – got the best response from study participants.

Another thing to keep in mind when it comes to audience-referencing headlines is the self-centered nature of the primitive brain.[61] Every audience, no matter how sophisticated, is asking, "What's in it for me?" A headline like this tells them.

How can you use this technique for your own writing? You might take a page out of KISSMetrics' book and use a headline like this one:

17 Advanced Methods for Promoting Your New Piece of Content

This headline combines two of the techniques we discussed. It uses a number – and an unexpected one at that – and it also addresses the audience directly by talking about "your new piece of content." All you need to do is think about how your content relates to the audience, and then put the audience in your title.

These techniques are all backed by science and using them can have a profound effect on the way people perceive and consume your content, whether it's on your website, in an email, or on social media.

Psychology of Sales and Marketing Emails

The next element of persuasive writing we will discuss is how to write persuasive emails. It is important to note here that many of the techniques in this section may also be applicable to writing intended for your blog, web pages, or social media accounts. We'll start with some general things to keep in mind, and then move into the science of persuasion.

Personalization

The first thing to keep in mind – and this relates to what we just discussed about audience referencing – is that an email that's personalized in some way is more likely to be read than one that's not. There are different ways you can personalize emails. Here are just a few:

- The first and most obvious method of personalization is to use your subscriber's first name. This is something that politicians do very successfully.

- You can also consider using a subscriber's purchasing history or background to personalize emails. For example, a business client who used your legal services to incorporate might want to hire you to help them with another common issue. You might say something like "We helped you incorporate. Now let us help you with _____."

- Other personalization possibilities include a client's geographical location, local weather patterns, and previous responses to emails. For example, if you know that someone on your mailing list hasn't been responding to previous inquiries, you might say, "What can I say to convince you to respond to our survey?"

Persuasive Writing Techniques

Now let's talk about some specific persuasive writing techniques you can use in your emails to make them more effective – and get a better response rate:

- The first thing to keep in mind – and this applies to every one of the scientific principles we'll discuss in this section – is that the tone of your writing is very important. A conversational tone that addresses readers directly (not coincidentally, like the tone I'm using in this book) is more persuasive than a dry or academic tone. It's hard to be persuaded of something if you feel like the writer's not talking to you. Regardless of what other techniques you use, remember that you're talking to a person, not a machine.

- The Rhyme-as-Reason Effect is a powerful cognitive bias that can help persuade people to accept what you say as trustworthy and accurate. This phenomenon was first identified by researcher Matthew McGlone in 1998.[62] In his study, he presented participants with familiar aphorisms in their traditional, rhyming form (Woes unite foes) as well as in a less-familiar, non-rhyming form (Woes unite enemies.) While participants found that both statements were true, they believed the rhyming statements more than they did those that didn't rhyme. Another example of this in popular culture is lawyer Johnny Cochran's statement during the OJ Simpson trial: If it doesn't fit, you must acquit. You can use the Rhyme-As-Reason Effect in your emails by including subtle rhymes when you make important points. A related technique is the Fluency Heuristic, which says that people's perception of facts is affected by how fluently they are expressed.[63]

■ A psychological principle that's similar to the Rhyme-As-Reason Effect is the Bizarreness Effect. The Bizarreness Effect – first identified by researchers Mark McDaniel and Gilles Einstein in 1986, says that people do a better job of recalling information that's bizarre or unexpected.[64] It's not the bizarreness itself that's memorable. Rather, the inclusion of something bizarre makes the information conveyed distinctive. In a follow-up study with Christopher Macklin, McDaniel found that including a distinctive or unexpected noun in a sentence greatly increased the chances that people would remember it.[65] Let's look at an example from the Foolish Adventures podcast:

Noah Kagan Loves Tacos And Teaching Entrepreneurs – FA190

What do tacos have to do with entrepreneurs? Nothing, really, but the bizarreness of the word's inclusion makes it memorable. How can you incorporate this technique into your emails? You don't want to overdo it, but try picking out the most important tidbit in your email – the one thing you want people to remember – and replace one of your words with something unexpected. Instead of saying that making a mistake could be detrimental, say that it would be cuckoo or bananas – anything to make it stand out from the rest of your writing.

- The Primacy and Recency Effects are two cognitive biases that go hand-in-hand. A pivotal 1962 study by Bennet Murdock showed that when people are presented with a list of objects or concepts, they remember the items at the beginning and end of the list more accurately than they do what's in the middle.[66] If you're presenting a long list of things in an email, put the most important things at the top and bottom of the list. It's also important to note that the longer the list, the lower the primacy effect becomes.

- In the chapter about conversion optimization, we talked about the Von Restorff Effect as it relates to color. Now let's talk about how to use it in persuasive writing. To refresh your memory, the Von Restorff Effect is a cognitive bias that prejudices us in favor of images and words that stick out.[67]

It's related to the Bizarreness Effect, but it's a little different in that the item in question only has to be different from what surrounds it. The example I gave you earlier had to do with changing the color of the button on a web page from green to red. You can use the same technique to make a particular word or sentence stand out. The Von Restorff Effect is the reason magazines pull out quotes and highlight them in the middle of a long article. Remember, we're more inclined to remember content at the beginning and the end of a long piece. The Von Restorff Effect is a way of counteracting that by highlighting something in the middle. To use the Von Restorff Effect in your digital marketing, look for opportunities to make content in the middle of what you're writing distinctive. In a long email, that might include **bolding** or *italicizing* chosen text, or using a different font or color.

- Regardless of who your clients are, Social Proof is important to them. The earliest study on social proof was conducted by Muzafer Sherif.[68] In it, he studied participants' interpretation of the movement of a dot of light. (The light was not moving but appeared to due to the autokinetic effect.) What he found was that individual responses varied but were consistent for each individual. However, when the participants were grouped together, they came to a consensus about the movement of the light before giving a response. How does this translate to your marketing efforts? It demonstrates a strong need for conformity and social acceptance. You can use it in your persuasive writing by letting your readers know how many times your content has been shared, or by including things like client testimonials. Even a simple statistic can do a lot to help you take advantage of social proof. Look at this image from Marketo's website:

You can see that their guide has been viewed 19,000 times. That's probably all the social proof a visitor to their site needs to convince them to fill in their information and download the guide. This type of statistic can be just as effective in the middle of an email or blog post as it is here.

- The Scarcity Principle is related to and often goes hand in hand with social proof. Human beings are hard wired to assign more value to something that is scarce than they are to something that's abundant. Scarcity is one of Cialdini's six Principles of Persuasion, as we discussed in the chapter about conversion rate optimization. A 2014 study looked at the perception of scarcity in several different ways by observing consumer behavior at a store that sold wine.[69] In the study, consumers were convinced of a wine's scarcity by two different methods. The first involved the salesperson telling them that the wine was exclusive. The second was indirect and occurred as a result of using empty shelf space to indicate the wine's popularity – note the connection to social proof. You can use the principle of scarcity in your digital marketing efforts by using phrases that highlight scarcity, things like "Act now" or "For a short time, we are offering..."

- Most people are familiar with the term "reverse psychology," to the point where it might almost be viewed as a joke. However, the theory behind reverse psychology is actually sound. It's linked to a psychological principle called reactance, which says that as a rule, people are inclined to dislike the feeling of their freedom of choice being curtailed in any way.[70] It's important to be careful when using this particular principle because so many of us are familiar with the idea of reverse psychology. However, used in subtle ways it can be very effective. How can you use it in your digital marketing? You might use phrases like, "I'm not sure you'll believe me" or "I'd love to try to convince you, but I don't think it will work." Those are subtle because the reversal is aimed at you, not at the client.

All of the above principles can be very effective persuasive writing tools if you use them properly. The key is to find ways to adapt them to your particular service or product.

Layout

We already talked quite a bit about design and layout in the chapter about the psychology of web design, so I won't spend too much time on the topic here, but there are a few things you need to keep in mind when writing marketing emails.

The first thing to remember is that, just as it was in web design, white space is important here. Nobody's going to read a dense email with no paragraph breaks – that's just common sense. However, there is science to back up the importance of having the proper layout for your emails.

The first study I want to tell you about is from 2004, and it looked at two things, reading speed and reading comprehension.[71] The study tested four different page layouts, with the primary difference being the inclusion or omission of a white space margin around the text being read. What they found was that reading speed was faster when there was no margin, but reading comprehension was higher and readers felt less fatigue when reading the text that included a margin.

The second study, which appeared in Usability News, examined the overall layout and how it affected reading speed, comprehension, and reader fatigue.[72] They presented two options, one page with optimal layout, and one page with suboptimal layout. The page with optimal layout included things like indentations, subheadings, and image placement. What they found is that the optimal layout did not improve reader comprehension of the content. However, it did greatly affect the participants' response to the text. On the whole, they found that the text with optimal layout was more satisfactory to read, and they had a higher degree of confidence in their level of comprehension of the material.

The marketing takeaway here is that formatting matters. It's just as important for emails as it is for web pages or any other digital content you might produce. If you are going to send marketing emails – especially long ones – then you would do well to include margins, subheadings and paragraph indentations to enhance the reader's experience.

Colors

Like layout, we talked about colors in the chapter about web design, but I do want to say just a few words about the psychology of using colors in marketing emails.

Let's start with the basics – should you use color in your emails? A 2006 study at the University of Tel Aviv showed that use of color in emails increased the probability that people who read the email would take the desired action by .2%.[73] That might not seem like much, but any increase is worth exploring.

On a practical level, the colors you use in your email should be consistent with your brand. If your firm's logo is green, then using the same shade of green in your email makes sense because it creates consistency in your marketing efforts.

It's also important to keep in mind that, while it can be difficult to predict an individual's response to a particular color, there are some preferences that appear to be universal. A 1994 study in the Journal of Experimental Psychology revealed that people overwhelmingly associate the color blue with positive experiences.[74] That makes it a good choice for your emails. Just make sure to use color sparingly. On the whole, overuse of color is a bad idea. That's especially true with colors that elicit a strong emotional response, like red. Overuse of red will not only agitate the person reading the email, it may lead to your email being marked as spam.

Images

The final email design element I want to talk about is the use of images. I already touched on this topic, but I want to take a minute to talk about how images can affect the way people respond to your marketing emails. A 2002 study showed a direct correlation between use of images in emails and conversion rates.[75] You already know that the brain processes images much faster than it does words, so adding a few well-chosen images to your marketing emails can help underscore the information you're trying to convey.

Psychology of Writing for Web Pages

Many of the psychological principles I have mentioned previously are applicable to writing content for web pages. However, since the goal of most web pages is slightly different from that of emails, I do want to discuss a few particular principles that I feel are especially effective for the persuasive writing that will appear on your website.

Creating a Common Enemy

Human beings have an inherent need for coherence in their lives. A 2010 study at the University of Kansas examined one way we attain that feeling of coherence: by identifying common enemies.[76] It turns out that psychologically speaking, we need enemies. They help us to accept the fact that we don't have control over everything that happens in the world around us.

How does this apply to digital marketing? Well, you can use the persuasive writing on your website to create the specter of a common enemy, something that you and your potential client can face together. Let's look at an example – this is from a tax attorney's website:

Most of our tax clients don't know they've done something wrong until suddenly they owe the IRS more than they expected, including penalties and fees. As your tax attorney our objective is to appease the IRS while keeping your finances solvent.

Note that this bit of writing does two things. First, it absolves the client of deliberate wrongdoing (they don't know they've done something wrong.) Second, it unites prospective clients and the law firm against a common enemy – the IRS. That's a very powerful persuasive writing technique. Regardless of what industry you're in, you can find a common enemy.

Fear of Missing Out

Nobody likes to feel that they're missing out on an opportunity or experience. We want to belong. A 2012 study that appeared in the *Journal of Personality and Social Psychology* examined the reactions of volunteers in response to an article written by an advanced math student.[77] Some of the participants were given a biography for the author indicating that they shared a birthday. After reading the article, all of the participants were given an unsolvable math problem. The study found that the people who believed they had something in common with the author worked longer on the problem than the control group.

Let's talk about how you can apply this need for belonging to your digital marketing. People crave community, so anything you can do to enhance the idea that your company will provide them with that can help boost your digital marketing efforts. This principle is closely aligned with both social proof and scarcity. The easiest and most obvious way to use the fear of missing out is by coming right out and saying something like, "Don't miss out on this opportunity" or something of that nature. If you prefer a more subtle approach, you could imply that your client would be missing out if they fail to do what you want them to do without actually coming out and saying it. For example, "Companies who use our services save 25% more on their taxes than companies who go elsewhere."

Immediate Gratification/Pleasure Principle

A psychological concept that's frequently used in digital marketing is the human need for immediate gratification. The most famous study of this phenomenon is known as the Stanford Marshmallow Experiment. Conducted in 1970 by researchers Walter Mischel and Ebbe Ebbesen, the study examined the reactions of pre-school aged children who were presented with two options.[78] The first involved receiving an instant reward of some kind of treat (most commonly a marshmallow although cookies and other treats were used as well.) The second involved the opportunity to wait and receive a more desirable treat at a later time. What the study found was that some children ate the marshmallow immediately while the remainder attempted delay. However, of the majority who chose to attempt the delay, only one third succeeded. The conclusion is that the draw of immediate gratification is very strong.

A related concept is the Pleasure Principle, first identified by Sigmund Freud in his writings about the id.[79] His theory is that pleasure-seeking is an immature id-based behavior, and that one hallmark of maturity is the ability to delay gratification.

Incorporating these two principles into your digital marking is relatively easy. Including a few key words that trigger the human need for immediate gratification can be enough to trigger potential clients to take action. Words that can help include:

- Quick

- Immediate

- No waiting

- Instant

For example, you might say, "Sign up now and get an immediate response."

Storytelling

The final principle we'll talk about in this section is storytelling. Our brains are highly attuned to stories. They trigger an emotional reaction.[80] Remember what I said earlier about the mammalian brain? Any digital marketing strategy needs to appease the mammalian brain after satisfying the reptilian brain.

An example of this principle in action is the Significant Objects project. The project is a social experiment run by Joshua Glen and Rob Walker.[81] In it, they obtained inexpensive objects and asked writers to come up with detailed stories that would explain the objects' significance. What they found is that people were willing to spend far more to obtain objects that they felt were significant than they were to get the same objects without a story attached.

To use this principle in your digital marketing, try crafting a compelling narrative on your web pages. You might prominently feature a client's personal story or even tell your own story in a way that will interest and engage your clients.

The Psychology of Calls to Action

The final element of persuasive writing I want to talk about is the psychology of the call to action. Your web pages and marketing emails all need to have one, and it's important to choose the right wording to get the results you want. Sure, you could go with a simple "Sign Up" or "Click Here", but the five concepts here will help you get better results:

- Perceptual set theory is a principle that tells us that people see (and read) what they expect to see. One experiment that demonstrated this involved presenting participants with non-words such as "sael."[82] Participants who were primed to see words associated with animals interpreted it as *seal*, while those who expected words related to boats saw it as *sail*. How does this relate to your call to action? Well, when they're visiting a web page (or reading a marketing email, for that matter) people expect to see a call to action. Make yours obvious. That doesn't mean it needs to be huge and bright red, but it should look like a call to action. It's also a good idea to make sure that your page flows in a logical way and that the CTA appears at a natural place in relation to the rest of your content.

- We already talked about the importance of creating curiosity in writing headlines, but it can apply to calls to action as well. One study that demonstrated the power of curiosity involved playing a faulty recording for the study's participants.[83] The researchers noted increased muscle tension and stress when the subjects were unable to hear the recording. To use this idea in your call to action, try telling your customers that they'll get trade secrets or unique information if they click your CTA. For example, you might say something like, "Click here to get insider tips."

- Another thing the human brain is hard-wired to do is to

anticipate positive outcomes. It turns out we're naturally optimistic and we want to anticipate good things happening to us.[84] You can make use of this desire in your CTA by describing what clients can expect to happen after they click the CTA in the most glowing terms possible. For example, you might say, "Click here to save thousands on your taxes." A statement like that can create a powerful level of anticipation and make your CTA irresistible.

- Another way to make your CTA more compelling is to make it the climax of a story that you tell on your page. Remember how powerful stories were in the Significant Objects study? Narratives are a powerful marketing tool because they help to arouse emotions.[85] You can use this principle by telling a story and then asking customers to click your call to action as part of the climax.

- Finally, you're probably familiar with Ivan Pavlov's famous reward-anticipation experiments with his dogs.[86] If you make your CTA sound like a reward you increase the chances that people will want to click on it. Everyone loves a reward. Try including a subtle compliment and implying that your CTA is a reward for a job well done.

Your call to action might not seem like a very big part of your web page, but it plays a key role in getting prospective clients to convert. Make yours as compelling and unique as possible by choosing the right words to accompany it.

Wrapping Things Up

Writing persuasive web content is a skill like any other, and it takes a lot of time to hone. It takes practice. However, the principles outlined in this chapter can go a long way toward helping you write persuasively for your blog, website, or email campaigns.

One of the best ways to shortcut the learning process is to build what digital marketers refer to as a "swipe file." Pick out websites you think have used persuasive writing effectively and bookmark them. Study them. Try to emulate their style and word choice. Rewrite them word-by-word, and analyze each as you go (don't plagiarize -- this is just an exercise for practice in deconstructing the elements of persuasive writing.)

It can be tricky to find good examples of landing pages online because without some sort of guidance, you just have to bounce around until you find a good one. One way to make the process easier is to look at a site like Unbounce, which helps people set up effective web pages. They've got a whole page on their site dedicated to examples of successful pages they've set up:

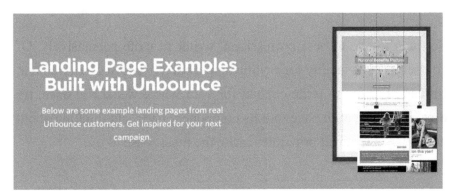

It can also help to subscribe to mailing lists of other companies in your industry to get a look at how they're using persuasive writing to market themselves. Even though we're concerned here with digital content, looking at print ads can be instructive too. Good advertising uses the same principles whether it appears in print or in digital form. A great source of tremendous ads is the *National Enquirer*. While this tabloid's circulation figures have declined in recent years, a good number of people still pick it up. Other tabloids are widely read, too, even if people might not openly admit it. If you feel ashamed at the thought of picking these up to flip through the ads, check out the ads that are running in publications like the *New York Times* and *Wall Street Journal*.

One of the keys to using persuasive writing effectively is to remember that every single written element in your digital marketing plan, whether it's the title of a blog post, the subject line of an email, a story you tell on your website, or the words you couple with a call to action, must work together to persuade your prospects to engage your services or buy your product. The goal is not to manipulate, but to understand the way the human brain works and how the words you write act upon it.

You don't have to be a professional writer to write persuasively. Of course having a facility for writing helps, but it's hardly a requirement. Instead of trying to write content for your whole website at once, try breaking down each page into its component parts and thinking about which psychological principles make the most sense to use.

Not every website will benefit from using every concept presented here. That's where common sense comes in. The goal of persuasive writing is (no surprise) to persuade. The tools that work on a customer who's shopping for a new car may overlap with those of someone looking to hire a lawyer, but there'll be differences as well. That's where understanding your customer personas can help. The content in your digital marketing campaign must be tailored to capitalize on the psychological triggers that best fit your target customers.

Key Takeaways

Over 60% of your potential buyers will read the headline only. Make sure that you spend time crafting an effective message.

The goal of every headline is to get readers to take the next step.

"Free" is a very powerful tool of persuasion.

Some techniques to use that can help you write persuasive headlines include:

- *Surprise readers with an unexpected word or concept*

- *Use negative superlatives to capture attention*

- *Use numbers – the higher, the better*

- *Incite curiosity and reward anticipation*

- *Use specificity to let readers know what to expect*

- *Reference the audience directly*

Personalizing emails using a customer's name or past purchasing behavior makes it more likely they'll read the email.

Persuasive writing techniques to use in emails include:

- Use an easy-to-read, conversational tone

- Use subtle rhyming or clever wording to make things more memorable

- A bizarre word can help to draw attention to important information

- Put important information at the beginning and end of your email

- Use the Von Restorff Effect to highlight important information in the middle of your email

- Offer social proof to convince customers to respond

- Invoke scarcity by using limited time offers

- Use reverse psychology and reactance sparingly

When it comes to layout, white space, limited use of color, and effective images can make your email more readable.

Persuasive writing techniques to use on your website include:

- Creating a common enemy

- Creating a fear of missing out

- Offering instant gratification by using words like quick, immediate, etc.

- Telling a great story to arouse customers' emotions

Make your call to action more effective by making it stand out.

Remember that an effective call to action arouses curiosity, creates anticipation, or serves as the climax to a story.

CHAPTER 5

THE PSYCHOLOGY OF PAID ADVERTISING

"Advertising people who ignore research are as dangerous as generals who ignore decodes of enemy signals."
~ *David Ogilvy*

Now that we have discussed the psychology of persuasive writing as it applies to your website, emails and other digital marketing materials, it's time to take on a new and related topic: paid digital advertising. Persuasive writing is, of course, just as important when you're writing ads as it is when you're writing blog posts or content for your website. However, there are some challenges that are unique to digital advertising, and they're what we'll talk about in this chapter.

The primary difference between the persuasive writing we discussed in the previous chapter and paid advertising is that, in many cases, persuasive writing may not involve a direct appeal to get customers to make a purchase. With paid advertising, that's not the case. The goal of a paid ad, whether it's an ad that appears on a search engine like Google or Bing, a paid ad or boosted post on Facebook or Twitter, or a remarketing ad aimed at customers who've visited your site without converting, is always to make a sale or a conversion. That means the psychological principles that apply are a little different.

The goal of this chapter, then, is to help you understand how and when to spend your money on paid digital advertisements. We'll start with the psychology of search. Most people who find your company online will find it using a search engine – and that means you'll probably spend some of your budget using Google AdWords. The only way to make search engine advertising work is to understand how and why people search for your company – and the specific words they're most likely to use to do it. I'll also tell you how to use your ad to answer a customer's question, and why it's important to look at your ad as the entryway to your website.

Next, we'll dig into the psychology of remarketing. Remarketing can be a very effective form of digital advertising, but it's important to use it properly. We'll talk about how and when to use remarketing, and then I'll give you a rundown of some essential psychological principles that will help you make your remarketing campaigns more effective.

The last type of paid advertising we'll talk about is paid social media advertising. Sites like Facebook and Twitter offer some intriguing advertising opportunities that give advertisers access to rich psychographics they can use to target ads at the people who are most likely to purchase their products or services.

Nothing's more frustrating than laying down money for paid advertising that doesn't earn you a return on your investment. With the information in this chapter, you'll have all the tools you need to ensure that your paid advertising gets the results you want.

Google AdWords

One of the most popular digital advertising options available is Google AdWords. Google is the world's largest search engine. From a budgetary perspective, the thing that's appealing about AdWords is that it's a pay-per-click system, which means you only pay when searchers click on your ad. However, the focus of this section will be on the psychology of using AdWords.

The Psychology of Search

Let's start by talking about why people go to Google and type in a keyword. As Brad Geddes points out in his book, *Advanced Google AdWords*, search is not the same thing as browsing the web.[82] People don't use Google to browse – they use it to find information. They're looking for something specific. They've got a problem or a question, and they type in the words that they think will get them a solution or an answer.

What you must remember when using AdWords is that your goal is not to convince Google to display your ad. Your goal is to make sure that when people type in your chosen keywords, your ad provides the answer that they're looking for. If it doesn't do that, they won't click it. It's as simple as that.

That takes care of why people search, but before we move into talking about the psychology of keywords, let's talk briefly about how they search. According to Geddes, it's important not to think of keywords as words per se.[83] Instead, psychology tells us that they are thoughts translated into words. The searcher has a question or problem, and the words they type in are their best attempt to translate their thoughts into words that will get them the results they want.

Picking the Right Keywords

You understand now why people conduct searches, and the next step is to choose the right keywords. With Google AdWords, you bid on selected keywords. For your ad to reach the people you want it to reach, you need to choose the best possible keywords.

Let's start with common sense. A lot of advertisers make the mistake of choosing the keywords that they would use. That's the wrong approach to take. When you're selecting keywords, your focus needs to be on your potential clients and what terms *they* are most likely to use. Think back to what I said earlier about customer personas. The work you do analyzing your customers can and should help you choose the best keywords.

The next thing to consider is the gender of your typical client. The Center for Reading Research did a study in 2014 to examine gender-based differences in vocabulary.[84] What they found is that, in general, vocabulary knowledge tends to fall along fairly traditional gender lines. For example, men are more likely than women to know and use words related to technology, science, and transportation. Women are more likely to know and use words related to art, flowers, and fashion.

How can you use this information? Well, if you're marketing mostly to men, and you sell a high-tech product, then using scientific and technical terminology in your ad may be fine. However, if your potential clients are evenly split in terms of gender, you should probably tone it down a bit and use keywords that are a bit less technical because women are less likely to search using them than men are.

It's also important to keep regional dialects and spellings in mind. A person in the United States who needs legal representation will search for a *lawyer* or possibly an *attorney*. A person in the UK might use *attorney*, but they might also choose the word *solicitor*. The same goes for different regions of the United States. Let's use a simple example. In the Northeast, the catch-all term for a carbonated beverage is *soda* or *tonic*. In the Midwest it's *pop*, and in the South, it's *coke*.

The primary thing to remember when choosing keywords is that you're marketing to people, not machines. Your goal shouldn't be simply to get your ad to display on a list of search results. Your goal needs to be getting your ad to display *in response to a search for a keyword that your potential clients are likely to use*. After that, you can worry about how to get them to click the ad.

How to Make Your Ad the Answer to a Client's Question

After you have selected the best possible keywords – the ones most likely to be chosen by your clients – the next step is to make your ad appealing to them. Remember what I said earlier. A keyword is actually a question. The person who types in a keyword is looking for the answer to a direct question or an implied one.

To start, let's look at the four basic types of keywords, according to Geddes:[85]

- ■ Explicit keywords are words that specifically describe a product or service. For example, if someone has a problem with their car, they might search things like *car repair*, *auto repair*, *mechanic*, or *mechanic open on Sundays*.

- ■ Problem-based keywords are exactly what they sound like. Instead of looking for a particular product or service, the searcher types in words that describe a problem they're having. So continuing with the above example, they might choose keywords such as:

  o Brakes don't work

  o Steering wheel won't turn

The people who use these keywords may be looking for a mechanic, but the primary thing they're looking for is an explanation or solution to the problem they're having.

- ■ Symptom-based keywords are similar to problem-based keywords, but instead of describing the problem itself, they describe a symptom of it. For example:

  o Black smoke from tailpipe

  o Loud noise from engine

  o Brakes make squealing sound

These are subtle differences, but a person who's not knowledgeable about cars might be more likely to use one of these words than one that identifies the problem.

- Product names or part numbers are the final types of keywords. They're typically used very late in the buying cycle. For example, a person who's shopping for a new computer might use different keywords to compare their options, and then a specific product name when they're ready to buy.

Part of what you need to do is to think about the specific keywords you've chosen and then put the customer's intent into a question form. Once you've done that, the next step is to craft an ad that provides an answer to the question being asked. Let me give you a quick example before we move on:

Someone searches the keyword *brakes don't work.*

Identify the implied question: Who can help fix my brakes?

Answer it with your headline: We fix brakes fast.

We already talked about the psychology behind immediate gratification, so the headline example I just gave answers the question and adds a little psychological incentive to the mix by promising to do it quickly. Even though the keyword doesn't contain a word like "quickly" or "fast," it's a safe bet that the person doing the search doesn't want their brakes fixed slowly.

The AdWords Ad as an Entrance to Your Website

The final thing I want to talk about regarding AdWords is the connection between your keyword, your ad, and your website.

If they keyword is a question and the ad is the answer, what role does your website play? One way to look at it is that the ad is the simple answer to the searcher's question, and your website is the in-depth answer. When searchers type in a keyword, they do so with the expectation that they're going to find the answers they're looking for. If they don't find it, they'll experience an *expectation gap*.

A 2003 study of customer expectations in the service industry found that there was a wide gap between what customers expected and what service providers thought they expected.[86] If you choose the right keywords and understand what potential clients are seeking, you can make sure that your website delivers on their expectations. For example, if a customer does a search for a specific brand of computer, they're going to expect that any ad they click takes them to a page where they can find that computer. If your ad directs them to your home page, they'll be disappointed. You don't have to be a psychologist to know that it's not a good thing to have disappointment be the first emotion people experience when they visit your page. That's a great way to have them hit the back button on their browser and click another ad instead. Not only does it not make psychological sense, but it also doesn't make financial sense. When a potential customer clicks on your ad, you have to pay for the click. If your website disappoints them, it means you just paid for a click for no reason.

Using Google AdWords can be a very good way to get highly targeted and motivated traffic to your website, but you need to make sure to take all three parts of the search process into consideration:

- Keyword research – understanding the customer's question

- Ad wording – answering the customer's question

- Website – giving a more detailed answer or a way to get it (for example, calling you to set up an appointment)

If you think of each step as part of a continuum, you'll be sure to meet your customer's psychological expectations.

Remarketing

The next type of paid advertising I want to talk about is remarketing. Remarketing is advertising that targets a potential client or customer who's visited your website without converting. For example, it might include someone who added an item to their shopping cart but didn't buy it, someone who viewed a product without adding it to their cart, or someone who started to fill out your contact form to subscribe to your list or make an appointment and didn't complete the process.

There are many ways that you can set up remarketing campaigns, including Google AdWords, Bing, and other services that target search engines, social media, and other websites. It can be a very powerful way to convince potential customers to convert. You can also use email marketing to retarget customers. All of the remarketing methods rely on the use of cookies (digital markers) to identify targets for the marketing campaign.

How to Use Remarketing to Grab a Customer's Attention

In this section, I'll tell you about some psychological principles you can use to make your remarketing campaigns more effective. The goal of any remarketing campaign is to remind potential clients what they missed out on when they navigated away from your site without converting. There's research that shows that familiarity plays a significant role in a customer's comfort level with a brand.[87] Remarketing can help you take advantage of that by giving you an opportunity to re-engage customers with your brand in a way that increases their familiarity.

With that in mind, let's look at the psychology behind remarketing.

Novelty and the Reptilian Brain

One of the tricky things about remarketing, psychologically speaking, is figuring out how to walk the line between repetition (which is required for brand recognition) and novelty (which helps pique curiosity and engage the reptilian brain.) Ideally, your remarketing ads should manage to do both things at once. Seeing the name of your brand may be enough to reap the benefits of familiarity, but you need to provide your potential customers with something new, too.

A 1997 study that appeared in Brain Research examined the effect of exposing rats to various stimuli, including novelty and pain.

What the researchers found was that when they put the rats into a new environment (thus introducing novelty) the rats' brains released acetylcholine.[88] Acetylcholine is a neurotransmitter that's directly linked to arousal and anticipation of rewards.

A later study by researchers Nico Bunzeck and Emrah Duzel showed that the human brain has a similar response.[89] Exposure to novel images triggered the release of happy chemicals like dopamine in the brains of participants. Exposure to novelty also increased the participants' ability to process and learn new information.

What does that mean for your digital marketing – and for remarketing in particular? To begin with, your remarketing ads should not be identical to the original ad your prospect clicked. If it's exactly the same, you run the risk of having your ad turn into background noise. It's fine for part of it to be the same. For example, you might use the same image but change the headline.

In the chapter about persuasive writing, we talked at length about the Curiosity Gap and how making your prospects curious can help draw them in. The same is certainly true of remarketing. If you craft a headline that presents your prospect with something new and something familiar, you have a great chance of getting them to come back to your site and finish what they started.

Let's look at an example. This is a Facebook remarketing ad from crowdfunding site Kickstarter:

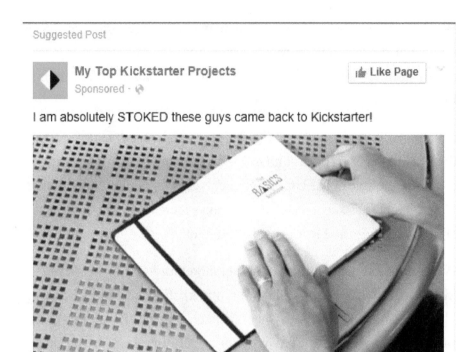

My Top Kickstarter Projects
Sponsored ·

👍 Like Page

I am absolutely STOKED these guys came back to Kickstarter!

This Will INSTANTLY Be Your Favorite Notebook...
The Features Stuffed Into This Planner: CRAZY!

It's like they found a solution for EVERYTHING!

WWW.KICKSTARTER.COM

What's effective about this ad? Well, for starters, it's a subtle remarketing ad. It's aimed at someone who visited the website without signing up for an account. It's not directly asking for any action but note the wording of the headline:

I am absolutely STOKED these guys came back to Kickstarter!

The two words "came back" are very effective, because they do a subtle job of implying that the person seeing the ad should do the same thing. The novelty comes in because instead of simply encouraging the target to come back to Kickstarter, they're highlighting the success of a specific project. The headline does a very good job of being familiar (including the Kickstarter name) and novel (highlighting a specific project.) It's very effective.

To use novelty in your own remarketing ads, try highlighting a benefit that's related to one your target searched previously, or putting a new twist on your services.

Justifications to Come Back

As human beings, we're hard-wired to want to justify and rationalize our actions. We have an acute ability to find justification for what we do. For example, one common cognitive bias is Post-Purchase Rationalization, which makes us find ways to rationalize the fact that we spent money on something even if the purchase decision itself doesn't seem rational.[90]

When you're writing a remarketing ad, it can be helpful to keep the human need for justification in mind. A 1998 study looked at justifications for criminal acts and found that there are two basic reasons people offer justifications: because their actions were right, or because they helped to avert a greater harm.[91]

That might not seem to apply to digital marketing at first, but it's important to take it out of the criminal context and look at it in a big-picture way. We want to believe, always, that our actions are justified. That includes everything from making a purchase to committing a crime.

To apply justification theory to your remarketing ads, you need first to accept that the people you're targeting failed to convert for a reason – something they also feel was justified. Maybe they had last-minute doubts about the quality or price of your product, or they just weren't ready to commit. The job of your remarketing ad, then, is to give them a reason to come back and finish what they started.

Some of the things you can do to help them justify a return to your website might include highlighting a particular benefit of your product or service or addressing a common objection, such as justifying the price of your product or emphasizing the lack of risk involved in buying it.

The Doppelganger Effect

We talked earlier in the book about customer personas, as well as the impact that using images of people who look like your customers can have. One very effective way to remarket to prospects is to use a psychological principle known as the *Doppelganger Effect*. In literature, a doppelganger is a person's double. Depending on the situation, the double may be supernatural or natural. One classic example from literature comes from Charles Dickens' *A Tale of Two Cities*.[92] The character Sidney Carton is a doppelganger of the main character Charles Darnay, and at the end of the book he takes his place at the guillotine.

Psychologically speaking, the Doppelganger Effect is a way of helping your customer to envision himself buying your product. A 2013 study in the Journal of Consumer Behavior[93] showed that consumers are inclined to mimic the behavior of other consumers when they perceive them as being similar to themselves.

How can you use this concept in your digital remarketing? You might try finding a photograph that features a person who has something in common with your customer. For example, a law firm that specializes in helping men deal with custody issues might use a photograph of a man and a child. An image like that can be very powerful and make it easier for a prospective client to visualize himself using the firm in question.

Contrast and Comparison

The next psychological concept you can apply to your remarketing efforts has to do with eliminating customer indecision by drawing clear contrasts between your product or service and those of your competitors. The human brain doesn't like ambiguity. We'd much rather take a known result – even if it's less than optimal – then take a risk on something that we can't predict. This preference is due to a cognitive bias called the Ambiguity Effect.

The Ambiguity Effect was first identified by Daniel Ellsberg in 1961 in a study published in the Quarterly Journal of Economics.[94] He conducted an experiment in which participants were presented with an urn containing a total of ninety balls. Thirty of the balls were red while the remaining sixty balls were yellow or black. They were given no information about how many of the balls were yellow or black – they knew only that 60 of the balls were one of those two colors. They were given a choice between two gambles. In the first, they would win $100 if they picked a red ball from the urn. In the second, they would win $100 if the ball they chose was black. The majority of participants chose Gamble A (the red ball) in spite of the fact that their chances might actually be better if they chose the second option. They preferred the certainty of knowing their chances (one in three balls were red) over not knowing.

How can you use the Ambiguity Effect in your remarketing efforts? You can start by thinking about how you presented the information about your product or service on your website. If you didn't draw a clear distinction to help prospects understand why they should choose your company over your competitors, a remarketing ad is a great place to do that. For example, you might highlight the fact that you offer a free consultation or mention your success rates in your headline.

The Small Yes (Consistency)

In the chapter on conversion rate optimization, I spent some time talking about Cialdini's principles of persuasion. One of those principles is the principle of commitment and consistency, and it's something that can be very useful in terms of effective remarketing.

One study that looked at commitment and consistency was conducted in 1968 by researchers Robert Knox and James Inkster at the University of British Columbia.[95] They studied people at a race track, asking them to assign a number value to how they felt their chosen horse would perform in the race. What they found was that bettors ranked their horses higher after placing a bet than they did immediately before they placed the bet.

Why? We have a deep-seated need to believe that our actions are consistent. When we say yes to something – as the study participants did by betting on a horse to win a race – we are naturally inclined to want the result to be consistent with our predictions.

A variation of this principle is something called the *Foot-in-the-Door Technique*. A 1966 study showed that people were more likely to perform a requested activity if they had already agreed to do something smaller previously.[96] The study group was asked to answer some survey questions about cleaning products, and the control group received no phone call. Two weeks later, everybody in the study received a call asking if someone could enter their home and catalog all the cleaning products they had on hand. Of the people who had received the earlier call, 52.8% agreed to the second commitment, while only 22.2% of those who didn't receive the call did so.

How can you use this in your digital marketing efforts? Well, one example might involve remarketing to people who signed up for your list but didn't make a purchase, or who put an item into their shopping cart but didn't complete the purchase. Instead of directly asking them to complete their purchase, you might target them with a remarketing email that asks them to answer a few survey questions. Anything you can do to get them to say "yes" to you in a small way will increase the likelihood that they'll make a bigger commitment later.

Another possibility to get repeat customers to come back is to send an email that reminds them about the earlier purchase they made. For example, look at this email from a hair products company:

WE MISS YOU

Extra 20% off to welcome you back - Simply click the shop now button below and enter code
MISSYOUHQ to activate your discount.
*Exclusions apply. Offer Valid until midnight 31st August 2015

SHOP NOW

This remarketing email does two things – it emphasizes past commitment and also addresses the pain of spending by offering a discount.

Pain Reduction

What effect does spending have on the brain? A group of researchers at Stanford University investigated that question in 2007 and came up with some interesting answers.[97] They gave shoppers $40 in cash and then did fMRI scans of their brains while showing them pictures of products marked with prices. What they found was that prices that the shoppers viewed as excessive activated the pain centers of their brains. In other words, human beings are hard-wired to be miserly.

If you're selling an expensive product or service, then, the goal of your digital remarketing campaign might be to offer potential customers some relief from their pain. For example, you might offer a coupon or discount, or – looking back at what we discussed earlier in regards to justification – find a way to make the pain of spending justifiable. Remember the remarketing email I showed you earlier? That's a classic example of reducing the pain of spending by offering a discount.

Perceived Progress

The final psychological concept we'll talk about regarding remarketing is perceived progress. A 2006 study that appeared in the *Journal of Marketing Research* showed that, as a rule, people tend to expend more effort they closer they are to achieving a desired goal.[98] For example, people who use customer reward cards (like the ones that earn you a free cup of coffee after you purchase ten cups) tend to make more purchases as they get closer to earning the free cup of coffee they expect when their card is full.

The study also found that people who received a card that required 12 stamps but had two stamps in place completed the reward program more quickly than those who received an empty, 10-stamp card. The number of purchases required to earn the reward was the same, but the perception of progress was enough to motivate the customer.

How can you use this tendency in your remarketing efforts? One way would be to use a headline in your remarketing ad or email that suggests that your target is very close to accomplishing what they set out to do. For example, a headline like, "You're almost there!" that redirects a prospect back to their shopping cart or partially filled-out form could be very effective. Note: you can only use this method if you set it up so that people don't lose the progress they made. If you make customers start over from scratch, there's a good chance they'll leave.

All of the above research shows that you shouldn't give up on a prospect just because they left your website without converting the first time. There are plenty of things you can to convince them to return. The key things to remember are that you need to understand why a customer abandoned a shopping cart or left your site in the first place, and then do your best to convince them to come back and finish what they started.

The Psychology of Social Advertising

The final type of paid advertising we'll discuss in this chapter is paid advertising on social media. Social media is an undeniable phenomenon – something we'll discuss in greater detail in the next chapter. Much of the marketing companies do on social media is content marketing, but there are good opportunities to use paid advertising as well.

The two social media sites where advertising is the most widely available are Facebook and Twitter. Both offer good – and relatively inexpensive – options for advertisers, including sponsored posts and Tweets, remarketing ads, and more.

Advertising on other social media sites is still in its infancy, but in the near future you may be able to advertise on sites like Pinterest and Instagram. For the purposes of this chapter, though, I will talk primarily about Facebook and Twitter and how you can use their unique platforms to make a psychological appeal to your customers.

Using Psychographics to Advertise on Facebook and Twitter

Marketing on social media is a concept that is growing more and more popular thanks to the new features that are being offered through the social media sites, such as targeted ads. This is a dream come true for a lot of marketers because it allows them to use customer profiling to reach the users who are most likely to want their products or services. The key to using targeted ads is that you need to target them properly. If you fall to make use of the segmentation and targeting tools that Facebook offers, for example, you'd be better off saving your money.

As with any advertising campaign, you need to make sure that you are targeting the right audience and reaching them when they're online to see your ads. The best way to formulate your Facebook ad campaign is to use psychographic segmentation.[99]

What Are Psychographics?

The first thing that pops into your mind when you hear psychographics is probably something that resembles an infographic – a visual representation of data. In reality, they are demographic statistics on steroids. It wouldn't really be fair to coin them as demographics, which typically include only data about age, sex, marital status, income, and other dry facts. That information has its place – and you can use it in social media targeting -- but psychographics take it a step further.

The difference between demographics and psychographics is simple. Demographics give you information about who your customers are. With a psychographic, you learn why your audience buys. Detailed psychographics can give you valuable insight into your customers' hobbies, habits, values, and spending habits.

Without the information provided from demographics and psychographics, you can't effectively reach your target customer. This is an excellent way to build buyer personas, which are detailed pictures of your customers and potential customers. Remember the customer personas developed by MailChimp? That's the type of thing you need to do to use social media targeted ads effectively. When you have a very clear and detailed picture of who your customers are, you can choose the proper psychographics to ensure that they see your social media ad.

To get a better idea of why psychographics are such a powerful marketing tool, let's look at an example. Note the differences between the demographic and psychographic information. This example is based on psychographic information for a nutritional counselor's target customers.

Demographic Info:

Female, married with kids, age 45-65, household income $100K+, may have diabetes or pre-diabetes, worried about weight gain, hormonal imbalance or lack of energy

Psychographic Info:

Wants a healthy lifestyle, but lacks time, goes online at night, especially to Pinterest, concerned about appearance and health, favors quality vs. economy, is fulfilled by family and career, values time spent with small group of friends

This should paint a good picture of why you need data from both sources. The demographic information gives you important information like gender, age, and income level; while the psychographic information can help you target your potential customers psychologically. With this insight, you can better target your ads to meet the needs of this persona. You can get this info by interviewing existing customers or investigating your website analytics. When starting your Facebook campaign, you'll be able to use the psychographics to specifically target your customers.

One of the best things about Facebook's psychographics is that you're not limited by choosing from a drop-down menu. You have the freedom to type in any interests, hobbies, or concerns you choose. Facebook may suggest additional keywords to you as you set up your ad. The demographic options are more limited, allowing you to set up age ranges, gender preferences, and other basic information.

Techniques for Social Advertising

Now that you understand how valuable psychographics can be let's talk about a few specific techniques you can use to make your paid social media ads more effective. Of course, many of the psychological studies and cognitive biases we have discussed so far also apply to any ads that you place on Facebook or Twitter, but there are some things that are uniquely suited to social media advertising.

Proximity and Positive Association

One aspect of social media advertising that's different from any other advertising platform is the fact that the ads you place there appear on a page that is closely identified with your customer's self-image. People use social media for a lot of different reasons, but the most common is that they want to share information about themselves – their thoughts, feelings, and opinions.

What does that have to do with advertising? Well, research shows that people who strongly identify with a brand or company are more likely to do business with that brand on an ongoing basis.[100] Identification builds loyalty. When you advertise on Facebook, your ad appears in one of two places: on the right-hand margin of the page (including on a target's profile page) or in the News Feed. Either way, your target's picture, name, friends, and other personal interests will be sharing space with your advertising.

What that means in terms of advertising value is that when you advertise on social media, you are buying brand identification. It's a lot easier for a person to identify with your company when they see it in a social context than it is when they see it in a neutral context, such as a search results page. The personal impact creates a positive association that can greatly increase the chances that a consumer will identify with (and buy) your product.

Customer Persona and Advertising

We've talked previously about the importance of customer personas, but I want to take a minute to talk about it specifically as it relates to social media advertising. Using psychographics can help you fine-tune your customer personas and decide which personas to target with a particular ad. For example, a company that sold natural beauty products might want to target women, but that's not a very specific persona. By segmenting the women they want to target, they might decide to run one social media ad targeting college-age women who are concerned about animal testing. A second ad might be aimed at women in their

40s and 50s who are mostly concerned about the environment and protecting their skin.

Whatever personas you develop, social media advertising is a great way to use advertising in a highly-targeted way that will appeal to the specific personas you develop.

Note: in the next chapter I will go into depth about the psychology of social media, and many of the psychological concepts in that chapter may apply to paid social media advertising as well.

Wrapping Things Up

Using paid online advertising is an important part of any online marketing strategy. There are a lot of different ways to spend your marketing dollars, and they require the same kind of psychological insight that you put into designing an effective website or email, or optimizing conversions.

There's no point in spending big money to buy ads for your chosen keywords on Google if you haven't done your research. Choosing the right keywords is as much a product of psychology as it is of economics. When you understand who your customers are and why they make the buying decisions they make, you'll be better able to determine which keywords to invest in.

Choosing highly-targeted keywords – the ones that are most likely to be used by your target customers – will get you the kind of traffic that yields a high return on your investment. If you don't use psychology to pick your keywords, you will in all likelihood end up paying for clicks from searchers who have no intention of buying from you.

The other thing that's important to remember about search engine ads is that each part of the process is on a continuum. The keyword your potential customer uses to search is the first step. The text and other information in your ad is the second step. The third and final step is your website – the page people less after they click your ad. Your website needs to fulfill their expectations, or they'll hit the dreaded back button and find another ad to click.

Remarketing is a very effective form of advertising that allows you to make use of several key psychological principles to get people who haven't converted to revisit your site. Again, they key is to understand why your target customer didn't complete their transaction in the first place and then use your ad to convince them that they should return to your site and finish what they started.

Finally, social media advertising provides some unique opportunities to help customers identify with your brand in a personal way. Because of the rich psychographics available to advertisers on social media, you have the option of targeting specific customer personas with ads tailored to their specific needs and interests.

Whatever type of paid advertising you choose, using psychology can help you get the largest possible return on your investment.

Key Takeaways

The goal of paid advertising is to make a direct appeal to the customer with the intention of getting them to convert.

The key to using Google AdWords effectively is understanding how and why people search. Searching is not the same as browsing. People search because they are looking for one of two things: the answer to a question or the solution to a problem.

The goal of advertising with Google AdWords is not to get your ad to display in response to your chosen keywords. It's to provide potential customers with the answer or solution they're seeking.

Use keywords that your target customer would use. Avoid industry jargon, and keep gender and geographical differences in mind.

Remember the four basic types of keywords: explicit, problem-based, symptom-based, and product-specific.

Always remember that your ads are aimed at people, not machines.

Remember that your AdWords ad is a gateway to your website.

The Google AdWords process is a continuum:

1. *The searcher asks a question by typing in a keyword.*

2. *Your ad answers the question and the searcher clicks on it.*

3. *Clicking leads them to your website, which provides*

a more in-depth answer and/or a way of solving the problem – by filling out a form, making a phone call, or making a purchase.

Both your ad and your website need to show potential customers what they expect to see. You don't want the first emotion they feel in response to your page to be disappointment.

Remarketing is a great way to increase brand recognition and familiarity.

The goal of remarketing is to target customers who have visited your site without converting.

Keep in mind the key psychological concepts that can help you plan effective remarketing campaigns:

- *Novelty*

- *Justifications to return to your site*

- *The Doppelganger Effect*

- *Contrast and comparison*

- *The small yes (consistency and commitment)*

- *Pain reduction*

- *Perceived progress*

Social media advertising provides you with rich psychographics that you can use to target ads to specific customer personas. Demographics tell you who your customers are, and psychographics tell you why they buy.

Because social media ads appear on your target customers' News Feeds or Timelines, they tend to identify strongly with the brands who advertise there because of their close proximity to things they identify with, such as their profile picture, friends, and other interests.

CHAPTER 6

THE PSYCHOLOGY OF SOCIAL MEDIA MARKETING

The most potentially transformative impact of social media is its ability to encourage brands to marry profit and purpose. The reason brands participate is that such outreach earns those companies social currency enabling them to start or participate in conversations that connect them to consumers in meaningful ways.
~ Simon Mainwaring

It wasn't that long ago that social media was a new thing – something being used by young people to communicate in ways that seemed trivial and alien to older people and businesses alike. That's no longer the case. It's not possible for any business, regardless of its industry or niche, to deny the power of social media as a way of connecting with customers, building brand recognition, and increasing sales.

Despite that fact, many companies are still using social media in a haphazard and ineffective way. The content that you post on social media has a direct effect on customers' perceptions of you as well as on the likelihood of their buying from you.

So let's talk about the psychology of social media. What are your customers expecting of you on social media, and how can you give it to them in a way that will get you the results that you want? In the last chapter, we talked about the close connection between social media and customers' personal lives, in particular the fact that social media advertising encourages your customers to identify with you in a way that other advertising doesn't. That's only one aspect of the psychology of social media use.

In this chapter, we'll start by digging into the psychology of why people use social media. As you might expect based on what you've already learned in this book, the answers are complex and deeply linked to the brain and its quirks. Some of the reasons have to do with the way sharing things about ourselves affects the chemicals in our brains while others have to do with emotions like empathy.

We'll also talk about brand personality as it relates to social media. I've already gone into the importance of creating customer personas, but a brand personality is different – it's who your company would be if it were a person. That might sound odd, but remember, you're interacting with people, not computers.

Finally, I'll tell you the specific psychological principles that you can apply to your social media marketing. Social media marketing is an act of persuasion, but the rules that apply to it are different because the medium is different.

Why People Use Social Media

Regardless of what type of business you have, the chances are good that the majority of your clients and potential clients use social media. There are over two billion active social media account worldwide, and that number is only expected to grow. Clearly, something about it appeals to people on a very deep level.

So let's start by talking about why people use social media. For the purposes of this book, I'm eliminating the reasons that have nothing to do with psychology, such as reconnecting with old friends and things of that nature. What does using social media do to the brain? Why is it such a big part of our lives? Let's start with chemistry.

Dopamine and Oxytocin

Why do people have such a hard time resisting the lure of social media? You might have heard people you know talk about social media addiction, or you might have observed that certain people have a very hard time staying away from Facebook for even a short period.

There's actually a chemical reason for that behavior. A 2012 study at Chicago University's Booth Business School measured participants' willpower as it related to a variety of things, including smoking, purchasing decisions, coffee drinking, and social media use.[101] Participants carried Blackberries and received signals from the researchers throughout the day. When they received the signal, they reported any incidents of craving or desire, including information about whether they resisted the desire or gave into it, and also rated the strength of the cravings they felt.

What the study found was that, as a rule, people had a more difficult time resisting the pull of social media than they did anything else, including cigarettes and caffeine. That flies in the face of what most of us believe about cravings and addiction. It turns out that social media use triggers the brain to release dopamine, a neurochemical that stimulates desire. In other words, Twitter is more addictive than drugs.

Dopamine isn't the only brain chemical involved in social media use. Oxytocin is the so-called "love chemical." Its release is triggered by a lot of different things, and it turns out that social media is an oxytocin-producing powerhouse. Researcher Paul Zak of Claremont Graduate University studies the effects of oxytocin on the brain. In one study from 2009, he induced the release of oxytocin by showing participants videos that aroused empathy.[102] Once their brains were primed for the rest of the experiment, he had them play a computer game that included making donations to other players. What he found was that the participants whose brains had been flooded with oxytocin were more generous than those whose brains hadn't been stimulated before they began to play.

Zak's studies on oxytocin and social media are ongoing, but he's not the only one who's noted the connection. A 2008 study showed that social activity such as the sharing that happens on Facebook triggers the release of oxytocin in both mice and human beings.[103] And a 2011 study by the Pew Research Center revealed that people who use social media sites like Facebook are more generous on average than people who don't, and that they have stronger social networks and more social support, as well.[104]

Self-Presentation

One of the most common things people do on social media is to (selectively) share information about themselves. The Facebook profile page, which shows users their pictures, profile information, and information that's been posted on their Timelines, is the clearest representation of how a user presents herself on social media.

What does that have to do with psychology? Well, a 2011 study showed that people who viewed their own profile pages on Facebook experienced an increase in self-esteem.[105] The participants were divided into three groups: the group who looked at Facebook, a group who looked in mirrors for the same amount of time, and a control group. What they found is there was no discernible change in self-esteem for the mirror and control groups, but that the Facebook group experienced a spike in self-esteem. In other words, using Facebook makes people feel better about themselves, at least when they're looking at their own profiles.

Social Currency

If you use social media, then you've probably experienced the rush that comes with posting something to your Facebook or Twitter account and having people respond positively to it. We all like validation and social media provides us with an easy way to get it.

Science backs up that feeling of pleasure we get from sharing on social media. Researcher Jonah Berger studies the content we share on social media and why some content goes viral and other content doesn't. His 2012 study, which was published in the Journal of Marketing Research, showed that content that inspired high emotional arousal – feelings of awe, anger, or anxiety – is far more likely to become viral than information that generates low-arousal emotions like sadness.[106]

What that translates to is this: when we post content that arouses emotions, we get a big response from our social media contacts. The response triggers the feeling that we have an impact on the world around us. In other words, it increases our social currency.

Reciprocity

I already told you about reciprocity, which is one of Cialdini's six principles of persuasion, in the chapter on conversion rate optimization. However, this is a cognitive bias that has a role in why we use social media, too, and it's related to social currency.

Getting "Likes" on Facebook or Retweets on Twitter strengthen our social connections – and that strengthening works in both ways according to a study that appeared in Psychology Today.[107] When we "Like" content that our friends post, it makes them see us as more empathetic and trustworthy. In return, that makes them more likely to reciprocate. The cycle of reciprocity serves as a way of deepening our social connections.

Shared Reality

Liking things isn't the only way we interact with people on social media. When we comment on content posted by friends – as well as on news stories – it helps to shape our perception of the world around us.

A 2005 study by Gerald Echterhoff, E. Tory Higgins, and Stephan Groll showed that our perceptions of experience are directly influenced by what our friends and social media contacts say about them.[108] In other words, the comments that we make on social media, combined with the comments we read from our friends and their friends, actually change the way we see the world. They help us form a sort of shared reality.

An interesting related study showed that negative comments that were polite had a greater chance of being taken seriously than those that weren't. The study looked at consumer reviews of products and found that people who read polite negative reviews might actually be more inclined to buy the product in question than they were before reading the review.[109] When it comes to social media commenting, politeness does matter.

The Looking-Glass Self

We already talked about the ways that using social media can boost the production of certain neurochemicals and improve self-esteem, but another reason that people use social media may be that it helps them to see themselves more clearly.

A 1979 study about how we see ourselves introduced the idea of the "Looking-Glass Self." What the study said was that we are not able to see ourselves clearly. We need input from other people in order to get a realistic view of ourselves.[110]

A more recent study from 2011 looked at the ways that online self-presentation affected the development of self-image in teenagers. The study, by researcher Shangyang Zhao, looked at how teenagers' online interactions differed from their real-world interactions.[111] He found that the way they presented themselves online played a significant role in the process of self-formation, even though there were differences in the way the represented themselves on the internet.

Obviously the concept of the looking-glass self is closely related to the other things we've discussed, including the way social media usage affects self-esteem and helps form our world views.

Empathy

A lot of our face-to-face interactions are guided by the fact that we mirror the facial expressions of the people in our lives. This mimicry is second nature and it helps to build empathy. How does that translate to social media?

Research shows that social media users found experts who used Emoji in their communications were more empathetic (and competent) than those who didn't.[112] Another study looked at the link between word choice, emoticon use, and social media influence. The study examined the content of more than 31 million Tweets and found that the most influential people were also the ones who were most inclined to use emoticons in their communications.[113]

In terms of why people use social media, what this means is that, in spite of the fact that social media communications happen in front of a computer screen, we crave personal connection and emotional interaction. We can achieve that connection through the use of carefully-chosen language and other emotional indicators such as Emoji.

Social Comparison

One aspect of psychology that drives us to use social media is social comparison. Social comparison is related to – but not exactly the same – as self-esteem. A 2013 study by Catalina Toma and Jeffrey

Hancock looked at how social media use affected the way we compare ourselves to others.[114] What they found is that students who viewed their own social media profiles prior to receiving criticism of a speech they had given were better able to cope with negative feedback than students who hadn't.

As a rule, people tend to be much harder on themselves than they are on their friends and family. Social media may help us to mitigate harsh self-criticism.

Nostalgia

The final reason that people use social media is because it stimulates feelings of nostalgia. When we reconnect with long-lost friends from childhood, share pictures of our childhood serves in community events like Throwback Thursday, and talk over past times, it makes reinforces our sense of who we are and what's important to use.

In the past, nostalgia was actually looked at as an illness. The term was coined by a 17th-century Swiss physician and closely connected to depression. However, a 2012 study actually showed that the opposite is true.[115] While feelings of nostalgia may initially be inspired by emotions such as loneliness and sadness, the act of looking back on significant events in our lives triggers positive emotions such as feelings of redemption and connection. It also strengthened social bonds and emotional connections between people who shared feelings of nostalgia.

From the studies above, it's clear to see that social media usage isn't driven merely by idle curiosity or boredom. The act of sharing information about ourselves, shaping our opinions, and seeing ourselves through the eyes of our friends and family offers deep psychological benefits. There's a reason social media use is so prevalent – and that's why you can't afford to ignore it in your digital marketing efforts.

In the next section, I'll talk briefly about brand personality before we move into the specific psychological tools you can use to create and share social media content that will engage your customers and help you attract new ones.

Social Media and Brand Personality

One of the most important things that internet marketers need to keep in mind when it comes to social media marketing is being true to your brand personality. We talked before about customer personas – and those are important on social media too. However, equally as essential is your company's persona. What is your brand, and what are customers expecting of you when they follow you on Facebook or Twitter?

Maintaining an active social media presence can do more harm than good if you aren't true to your brand's personality. For example, some B2C companies maintain a playful or humorous social media presence that helps foster an informal relationship with their customers. B2B companies may be more likely to adopt a formal tone. The most important thing to remember is that the tone you project – the "persona" posting your social media content – must be consistent with the view customers have of your company or brand.

Aspects of Brand Personality

The best way to understand brand personality is to think of the human traits your customers would assign to you. J. L. Aakers' study[116] in the *Journal of Marketing Research* broke down brand personality into five main traits:

- Excitement: carefree, spirited, youthful, imaginative

- Sincerity: genuine, kind, family-oriented, thoughtful

- Ruggedness: rough, tough, outdoorsy, athletic

- Competence: successful, accomplished, influential, a leader

- Sophistication: elegant, prestigious, romantic, pretentious

The key thing to keep in mind is that these traits don't just describe how your customers feel about your brand, they describe how they feel about themselves, too.

That's why understanding your brand's personality is so crucial, especially when it comes to social media. It's not just a question of knowing how your customers see you – it's knowing how they want to see themselves. When you know that, you can make sure that everything you post reflects that persona back to them. In other words, your social media page can reinforce their positive opinions of your company, and of themselves. If you do can do that, you'll be able to turn prospects into customers, and first-time customers into loyal repeat customers. That's the goal of any good marketing campaign.

To get a better idea of how your brand personality might affect your social media presence, let's explore some of the ways that a brand can demonstrate its personality.

Look

Just as you express your personality by choosing clothes and accessories that reflect it, a brand can represent its personality visually too. Some of the things we've already discussed play into the look of a brand's personality, such as the colors and fonts you use on your website. Your logo is an important part of how you present yourself visually, too.

What does this mean for social media? Well, for starters, you want to make sure that the visuals on your social media pages – especially on sites that lend themselves to visual content, like Facebook, Pinterest, and Instagram – reflect your personality. Look at this example from Red Bull, the energy drink company. They have a brand personality that's young and adventurous, and this video they posted certainly reflects that:

Note that the Red Bull name and logo are clearly visible on the zip liner's helmet and that the company has also used its logo as its profile picture. A lot of the content Red Bull posts features extreme sports and daredevil activities, like swimming with sharks or skydiving. The important lesson from that for any company is that their content isn't about their products, but it *is* about their brand and its personality.

Sound

The sound of what you post on social media is just as important a reflection of your brand personality as the way it looks. We've already talked a lot about writing and language, and many of the same rules apply to social media as apply to your website and emails. The tone of what you say on social media matters as much as the information you convey.

You'll notice that in the example above from Red Bull, they start the post by saying, "Jump, jump!" That a very informal writing style – it's energetic, youthful, and a little irreverent, which fights right in with their brand personality.

To get an idea of how much social media language can vary from company to company, let's look at another example from Rolls Royce, the luxury car company. Their Facebook page puts a lot of emphasis on their ability to create bespoke, or custom, cars for their customers. It's a luxury product, and the exclusivity of having a car that's unlike any other is very appealing to their customers, who also like to see themselves as unique and exclusive. Here's a piece of content that reflects that perfectly:

Rolls-Royce Motor Cars
July 14 ·

Where do you find inspiration? From the drama of architecture to the vivid colours of nature, we'll take your inspiration and hand craft it into a reality.
Bespoke is Rolls-Royce.

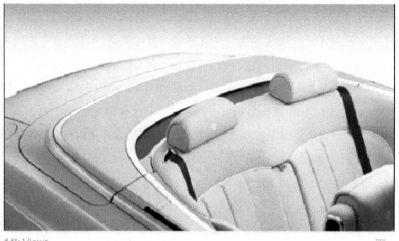

14k Views

The screenshot is actually a frame from a video that alternates between showing scenes of inspiration and the cars that resulted from that inspiration. Note that the language is far more formal than the language Red Bull used. It's also a little lofty and aspirational, both personality traits that are very much in keeping with the Rolls Royce brand.

Actions

A brand's actions matter as much as its look and its voice. When it comes to social media, your actions might relate to a number of things, including the way you respond to customers and the information you choose to share. For example, a company might choose to encourage their customers to engage in charitable activities or other social campaigns. Here's an example from Bank of America's Facebook page:

Bank of America
August 18 at 6:30am ·

All you have to do is say "Thanks" to help our service members and veterans. For each expression of thanks that you share using #troopthanks, we'll donate $1 – up to $1 million – to Wounded Warrior Project.

Here, they're presenting themselves as a brand that cares about America's service members and veterans. Notice that it's not just a question of words. The post expresses support for their troops, but they're backing it up with action and donating money to the Wounded Warrior Project. This post garnered over 1,200 Likes and almost 400 Shares, far more than most of the content around it. A post like this one can be a great ambassador for your brand.

The content you post on social media must be a true reflection of your brand's personality. If you take the time to thoroughly research your customers and understand how they see you, your social media pages will make them feel more connected to your brand – and more loyal to it – than they otherwise might.

How to Implement Psychology in Your Social Media Content

Brand personality is important, but the psychology of social media marketing involves more than simply having a consistent look and voice. In this section, will look at some studies on social media marketing and talk about how you can use the information they reveal to boost your own social marketing efforts.

Emotions, Especially Happiness Are Contagious

When it comes to social media, the emotions that users (including companies) express online are quite contagious. The posts displaying the strongest emotions spread like wildfire, which can be a great or devastating thing. Imagine a customer who's thrilled with your product or service writes a post that spreads -- that's something any company would love.

But what about a displeased customer who is angry with the experience or product/service that your business has offered? This also can spread rapidly (aka become viral) and be devastating to your business reputation. This phenomenon is part of why it's important to be involved in social media, so that you can keep track of what people are saying about your business.

One of the biggest social media studies ever conducted illustrates this point exactly.[117] The research was performed at the University of California at San Diego School of Medicine. It examined the emotional content of one billion posts on Facebook using software. The posts were made over the course of two years.

The results of the study were remarkable. What they showed was that the mood of Facebook users was directly affected by the weather – and not just in places where the weather was bad. According to the study, on gloomy rainy days, emotions that were displayed by Facebook users who lived there spread to places where it wasn't raining. In fact, every negative post they studied affected an average of one to two other people.

In case you're not convinced by those results, there was another Facebook study that was performed that shows similar evidence of emotional contagion.[118]

In this study, the focus was on negative emotion contagion, but it did find that positive emotions are significantly more contagious than negative ones. That's great news for Internet marketers. The negative contagion generated an average of 1.29 negative posts from friends, while positive contagion generated an average of 1.75 posts that were positive.

So how can you apply the information in these two studies to your social media marketing strategy? You can start by using a positive tone in your social media posts at all times. Your tone will have a direct impact on the way your customers feel when they see your posts.

Another way to make use of emotional contagion is not to put off responding to negative feedback from customers. The more quickly you address it, the easier it will be to put out the fire. Bank of America is a company that tends to see a significant amount of negative feedback on their posts, but it's obvious from their Facebook page that the address each complaint quickly. Let's look at a quick example:

 Beth Rogers Mohler Bank of America has horrible customer service!
Like · Reply · 👍3 · August 18 at 6:54pm

 Bank of America ✔ Beth, we are very interested in obtaining additional details so that we can better understand any challenges you may have experienced. We would like the opportunity to connect with you and offer our assistance once you provide details via our Get Help App at http://go.bofa.com/fbhelpdesk. ^eloy

 Bank of America: Get Help
Send a Service Specialist a private message. Get a reply in 1 business day.
SOCIALAPP.BANKOFAMERICA.COM

Like · Reply · 👍2 · August 19 at 7:40am
↳ View more replies

Note the positive tone of the Bank's response. There's no defensiveness or negativity, even though the customer's comment was very negative – and also not the type of thing that's easily addressed because it lacks specific detail. Another thing Bank of America does right here is to nip the complaints in the bud by moving the customer service process offline.

A good way to approach complaints on social media is to remember that every negative comment is an opportunity that you can turn around if you handle it properly – and keep it positive.

Your Profile Picture is Very Important

Whether you're a large corporation, small business owner or entrepreneur, the photo you choose for your profile should be well thought out. Sometimes using your brand or company logo for your profile pic isn't the way to go.

A study published in Psychological Science shows that social media users draw conclusions about profile pictures within 40 milliseconds of seeing a photo.[119] The researchers took photos of individuals with slightly different facial expressions, then asked participants to survey the photos based on competence, attractiveness, meanness, creativity, extraversion, trustworthiness, and intelligence.

Based on these photos, the participants changed their minds about their decision after seeing a slightly different photo of the same person. The photos show tiny variances in facial expressions from headshot to headshot, changing the view the participant has of a particular individual. What does that mean for your social media profile pictures? Well, depending on your business, you may want to consider using a personal photo. For example, someone who runs a business consulting firm might do well to feature a picture of himself instead of a logo. The personal touch can make a big difference. Companies who are looking to hire a consulting firm want to know who they're doing business with.

If you're not sure which profile picture will serve your company best, you can always do some A/B testing to find out.

Social Feedback is a Big Deal to Users

Earlier in the chapter, we talked about the fact that one of the main reasons that people use social media is to feel that they are part of a community. It should come as no surprise, then, to find out that social media users love to give and receive feedback. There was a study conducted by Dr. Stephanie Tobin from The University of Queensland's School of Psychology, which showcases that when there's active participation in social media, the users have a high sense of connectedness.[120]

In the study, researchers studied people who posted to Facebook frequently. They split the participants into two groups, and told half the group to stay active (meaning that they could share content and post on others' content) and the other half to simply observe the activity of other people without interacting. By the end of the study, the individuals who didn't interact on Facebook for two days experienced a negative effect on their personal wellbeing.

In another part of the same study, the participants were told to post on social media accounts, but the researchers made sure no one gave feedback or responded. The people who received no feedback were found to have reduced feelings of belonging and connectedness, as well as having lower self-esteem than the people who received feedback on what they posted.

How does this information relate to your social media marketing strategy? What this study tells us is that the people who use social media crave responses and feedback. It makes sense to respond to criticism, but it's also a good idea to thank customers for their comments. As long as you do it in a way that's consistent with your brand's personality, you can also take the time to join in on relevant conversations, provide opinions, and add value or fun.

Posts that Arouse Emotions Promote Social Sharing

One of the most important things that marketers need to understand about social media is that users are far more likely to share content that arouses an emotional reaction than they are to share neutral content. If you think about the types of things you typically see on social media, it's easy to believe that's true, but let's talk about the science behind it.

A 2011 study by Jonah Berger of The Wharton School studied the link between emotional reactions and social sharing. The theory he tested was that emotional arousal activates the nervous system, getting it riled up.[121] The act of sharing the source of our emotional arousal provides a sort of closure that releases us from this state.

In a double study, the participants in one group were given videos to watch that activated their emotions. To make sure that the results were not skewed by the type of emotion that was aroused, half of this group were given videos that aroused a positive reaction and half were given videos that aroused a negative reaction. The other group watched only neutral videos. In the second study, some of the participants sat still, while others jogged in place. At the end of the study, all of the participants were asked whether they would share a pre-selected article.

The double studies both showed that the participants who were in the first group were more likely to share. The joggers were more than twice as likely to share the article as the people who didn't jog. What's interesting about the second part of the study is that physical arousal had a very similar effect to emotional arousal, which indicates the involvement of the nervous system.

This study clearly demonstrates why the content you share on social media needs to be emotionally engaging. If you can make your customers feel a strong emotion, they are far more likely to share your content than they would be otherwise. By combining the information in this study with the information from earlier in the chapter about emotional contagion, you can see that sharing content that elicits a positive emotion is a good idea for any company that wants its content to be widely distributed and shared.

The Endowment Effect

The Endowment Effect is a cognitive bias that causes people to ascribe more value to items they already own than to items they have not yet acquired. Basically, the sense of ownership makes people assess a higher cost to things in their possession.

A 2000 study conducted by Dan Ariely and Ziv Carmon illustrated how dramatic the valuation of objects can be once ownership is conferred.[122] The study looked at the lottery system for basketball tickets at Duke University. Because the basketball program is so popular there, the university has a complicated lottery system in place to determine who gets tickets. After the lottery was complete, people who did not receive tickets were asked what the maximum price was that they would be willing to pay to get one. The average was $170.00. Contrast that with the people who received tickets, who were asked how much they would have to be paid in order to be willing to give up their tickets. The average price was $2400 – that's more than fourteen times as much!

How does this apply to your social media marketing? You can encourage existing customers to increase the sense of ownership they feel about your products by soliciting feedback and suggestions from them. Look at this example from car manufacturer Mercedes-Benz:

Enjoy our selection of the week's most liked Instagram shots. And while you're at it, why don't you head on over to Instagram and 'like' our channel or send us your best Mercedes-Benz shot via #MBFanPhoto to be featured on said channel? http://instagram.com/MercedesBenz

This is a great example of crossover social media marketing. They're sharing fan photos of cars from their Instagram account on Facebook and encouraging fans to submit more photos. That's a very effective way to encourage the Endowment Effect.

Conformity

Human beings have a deep-seated need to fit in and conform to societal standards. It's very hard to be the one who stands up to peer pressure. A 1956 study by Solomon Asch investigated this phenomenon by quizzing students on factual information.[123] Actors were intermingled with the students and instructed to give incorrect answers. The result was that even students who knew the correct answers agreed with the incorrect answers in order to blend in with their peers. A 2012 study looked at conformity and social media and found that the need to conform had a direct impact on consumers' purchasing decisions.[124]

How can you use the idea of conformity to bolster your social media marketing efforts? One way to do it is to get key influencers and industry leaders to share information about your product on social media. Also, encouraging comments and getting your followers to share stories about how they use their product can be a way of encouraging others to purchase it.

Mere Exposure Effect

The Mere Exposure Effect is a cognitive bias that makes people more likely to assign positive traits and features to things that they have been exposed to frequently. In other words, familiarity doesn't breed contempt – it actually breeds affection!

The original study on mere exposure was conducted by Robert Zajonc in 1968. In his study, he showed subjects a series of words, nonsense words, and symbols. What he found is that the more often a subject saw a particular word or symbol, the more likely he was to assign a positive meaning to it.[125]

How can you use the Mere Exposure Effect in your social media marketing? One way is to remember that it's not a bad idea to re-post helpful or compelling content. Obviously you don't want to overdo it, but you can find slightly different ways to share important information about your product or service and increase the chances that people will have a positive opinion of it.

Propinquity Effect

Another psychological principle that's related to the Mere Exposure Effect is the Propinquity Effect. This phenomenon was first studied in 1950 by researchers Leon Festinger, Kurt Back, and Stanley Schachter.[126] They observed groups of people living in small apartment buildings, and found that the proximity of living arrangements was the best predictor of whether or not people in the group became friendly with one another.

To use the Propinquity Effect in your social media marketing efforts, the best thing to do is to maintain an active presence on social media. When customers and potential customers grow accustomed to seeing your posts on their pages, they will also feel a closer connection to you and your products.

Buffer Effect

Nobody likes to feel stressed out or worried. One of the things that can help mitigate the effects of those harmful emotions is having a good support system in place. In fact, people who have positive support experience less stress than people who don't. It's a psychological phenomenon called the Buffer Effect.

One study that investigated the Buffer Effect looked at new mothers. One group had strong social support while the other did not. The group with strong support had fewer medical complications and lower levels of stress than the people who didn't have strong support.[127]

How can you apply this to your social media posting? One reason that people follow their favorite companies and brands on social media is to have an easy way to get in touch with them in case they need help or customer support. Make sure that you monitor your social media pages and respond quickly to customer questions and complaints. Customers who feel that you care about them are less likely to be dissatisfied than customers who feel that they've been overlooked.

Everyone Loves a Story

Human beings are hardwired to love stories. There's a reason that we spend so much of our time engaging with both fiction and narrative non-fiction. Reading and watching stories helps us to understand the world around us, and that's just as true on social media as it is anywhere else.

A 2008 study by Raymond Mar and Keith Oakley of York University examined the effect that stories have on the human brain.[128] What they discovered is that reading stories (their study focused on fiction) created a simulated social experience that helped study participants do a better job of processing real-life social situations. It also made participants better able to empathize with other people.

How can you use the human love of stories to market more effectively on social media? You can start by sharing stories about your company, including profiling leaders and employees or telling the story of the development of a product. Other options include encouraging customers to share their stories and then re-sharing them. A customer testimonial or case study can be a way of combining storytelling with positive information about your product or service.

Wrapping Things Up

No company can afford to ignore the power of social media as a way of marketing a product or service. Yet surprisingly, many businesses are not using social media to their best advantage. People want to connect with their favorite companies or brands, and if you're not giving your customers the opportunity to connect with you then you're missing a great opportunity.

Like any other form of digital marketing, psychology plays a big role in social media marketing. It's not just a question of posting occasional information about your product or service. People aren't looking for sales pitches from the companies they follow on social media. They're looking for connection, engagement, and value. When you understand who your customers are, as well as how and why they use social media, you can do a much better job of sharing content that that will entertain and engage them than you would otherwise.

Key Takeaways

Over 2 billion people – nearly a third of the world's population – use social media, a number that is only expected to grow.

Remember that there are specific reasons people use social media. For example:

- *Sharing things about themselves on social media triggers the release of happy brain chemicals such as dopamine and oxytocin.*

- *Social media usage and self-presentation are closely tied together.*

- *Sharing information on social media helps to increase our social currency and standing.*

- *Liking and sharing our friends' content on social media triggers reciprocity, which means we can expect to get a response.*

- *Sharing experiences with our social media contacts helps to shape our view of reality.*

- *Interacting with friends on social media helps to increase the capacity for empathy.*

- *Using social media can invoke nostalgia.*

Maintaining an effective social media presence means understanding your brand personality and how it also represents how your customers want to see themselves. Everything about your social media pages, including their look, sound, and the actions you take there, needs to be reflective of that personality.

Some of the most essential things to remember about social media are:

- *Emotions are contagious, and positive emotions are more contagious than negative ones.*

- *The profile picture you choose can have a big impact on the way people perceive your company.*

- *Content that arouses emotions is far more likely to be shared than neutral content.*

- *You can increase customers' valuation of your products by posting information about their features and sharing stories from customers.*

- *The more customers are exposed to your brand, the more they will like it.*

- *Social media provides emotional support to people who need it, and providing good customer support is a way of triggering the Buffer Effect.*

- *Stories are a great way to keep people interested and engaged with your content.*

Always keep the focus on your customers. Social media is not the place for a hard sales pitch.

CONCLUSION

Thank you for reading *Digital Neuromarketing*. The world of marketing has changed dramatically with the arrival of the internet and the emerging fields of neuromarketing and behavioral marketing. Keeping up with changing trends and new information can be a challenge, especially if the idea of linking marketing to psychology is new to you.

The human brain is remarkably complex and endlessly interesting. We all tend to think that we are highly logical creatures, and yet we are susceptible to scores of strange mental shortcuts and cognitive hiccups that influence our decision-making process. The mistake a lot of marketers make is in thinking that decisions are logical. They spend their time and energy crafting well thought out, rational marketing campaigns that don't have a prayer of succeeding because they fail to take their customers into consideration.

You might have noticed that one of the key points of this book, something that was mentioned many times over, is that a successful digital marketing campaign will always put the customer first. It's important to remember that marketers are just as susceptible to cognitive biases as anyone else. Indeed, there's evidence to suggest that knowing about cognitive biases doesn't do a thing to make us able to avoid them. That might seem counterintuitive, but it's true.

What that means is that, as a marketer, you're just as inclined to want to talk about yourself (or, in this context, your product or service) as any one of your customers. The danger of giving in to that temptation is that you can lose your customers' interest. They're not any more interested in hearing a laundry list of facts and figures about your product than you are in reading their grocery list.

In other words, this is one area where you must overcome your tendency to talk about yourself in favor of keeping the focus on your customer. Every aspect of your digital marketing, whether it's your landing page, email campaigns, blog, or social media pages, must be geared toward engaging and entertaining your customer. It's a hard thing for many people to accept, but when it comes to the psychology of online marketing, what you think doesn't matter. What your customer thinks is the whole ball game.

What are some of the key ways to keep the focus on your customer? Let's do a quick recap:

The Psychology of Marketing

Remember that your customer has three brains, and that in order for your digital marketing efforts to be a success, you must appeal to all three of them *in the correct order*. That means first dealing with the fear and survival-based reptilian, or old, brain. The reptilian brain is highly visual and has a very short attention span, so your primary focus must be on addressing your customers' fears or concerns quickly, and then offering a solution.

The mammalian, or middle, brain comes next, and that means thinking about your customers' emotions. You might appeal to emotion by telling a story or using visual content that arouses emotion. The middle brain is just as important as the old brain, and you won't be able to get to the final, most rational part of the brain until you have dealt with the middle brain.

Only when you have satisfied the reptilian and mammalian brains should you move on to the logical part of your sales pitch, the part that applies to the new, or rational, part of the brain. This is the part of the brain that can evaluate product features and prices. But even at the end of your landing page or email, you need to recap the key points for the reptilian brain. Remember, it will only recall the beginning and end of what you say, so make sure to bring things back around before you wrap up.

Other key things to remember about the psychology of marketing are:

- Human beings are very susceptible to a wide variety of mental shortcuts called cognitive biases. Understanding how they work can help you craft effective marketing campaigns, but you must be careful not to fall victim to them yourself.

- Don't forget to take behavioral psychology into account too. Remember that things like eye movements and reading habits will have a direct effect on how potential customers perceive your digital marketing campaigns, and tailor them to take advantage of those behaviors.

Conversion Rate Optimization

Too many marketers focus on attracting more traffic to their websites instead of paying attention to what matters – converting more of the traffic that you already have. There are only two ways to make more money online. The first is to increase traffic, and the second is to increase conversions. Increasing conversions is arguably both more effective and less expensive than increasing traffic.

Conversion rate optimization is a science, and it's essential to do research to determine what's working and what isn't. The science breaks down into three major components: the psychology of influence, the psychology of audience, and the psychology of design, content, and marketing. All three of these components are about the customer. Influence is about the things that affect your customers' thought process, such as cognitive biases. Audience is about who your customers are, and design, content, and marketing are about how your customer perceives each element of your digital marketing.

Cialdini's Principles of Persuasion can help you stay on track in terms of appealing to your customers. Remember that the six principles are: reciprocity, commitment & consistency, social proof, authority, scarcity, and liking.

Cognitive biases can play a huge role in conversion optimization and some of the ones that can have the biggest impact on your marketing efforts include:

- The Anchoring Effect

- Loss Aversion

- The Framing Effect

- The Illusion of Truth

- The Von Restorff Effect

- The Paradox of Choice

One of the most helpful things you can do to boost your conversions is to develop detailed customer personas. All of us like to see images of people who we relate to, and your customers are no different. When you know who they are, you can make sure to reflect the images they want to see.

Finally, the key to CRO is testing everything. It's important not to test more than one aspect of your campaign at a time, and to conduct the test for a long enough period of time that you can draw an accurate conclusion about how your customers are reacting to each option.

Web Design

Like CRO, web design is also all about your customers, and how they perceive the design choices you make. One of the best ways to keep the customer at the center of your design decision is to remember the design hierarchy of needs. If you put too much emphasis on making your website look good at the expense of the other needs, your customers will feel left out in the cold. The main things to remember are functionality, reliability, usability, proficiency, and creativity. Note that creativity, which includes the aesthetics of your website, comes last. That's not to say that it appearance doesn't matter, but it *won't* matter if your website isn't functional, reliable, and easy to use.

While functionality is more important that the aesthetic choices you make, that doesn't mean that aesthetics is unimportant. The images, colors and fonts you use can have a huge impact on the way customers perceive your website. For example, it's essential to choose colors that customers see as being harmonious with your brand. Functional products do best with functional colors – there's a reason that John Deere tractors are primarily green. Green is a functional color associated with growing things and farming, and John Deere sells farm equipment. Remember that when you're picking colors for your website.

The contrast between the colors you choose is also important. There's a reason most web pages feature black text on a white background – it's easy to read. If you get too off-the-wall with your color choices, you could end up scaring customers away.

The same goes for fonts. Readability needs to be your first concern, followed by the appropriateness of the font for your website. Most web designers prefer Sans Serif fonts. If you decide to use ornate or offbeat fonts, use them sparingly. They're fine in your logo or possibly in a headline, but you should never use them in the body of your content. Web users are notoriously impatient, and if it's not easy for them to read your content, they'll leave.

Finally, remember that every aspect of your design needs to be thought out with your customer in mind. That means avoiding the top design mistakes, the things that will make customers hit the back button on their browser and find another website. Those mistakes include having a cluttered layout, navigation that isn't intuitive, low-contrast colors or fonts that are too small, impenetrable blocks of text, too many calls to action, or outdated design. The primary goal of your website – and every part of your sales funnel – should be providing a seamless and intuitive experience for your customers. The easier it is for them to read and navigate your content, the more likely it is that they'll convert.

Persuasive Writing Fundamentals

The reptilian brain may get first shot at your marketing content, but the fact that it responds better to visual content than to written content doesn't mean that you can gloss over the importance of persuasive writing. Again, it's crucial to keep the focus on your customer, starting with writing a great headline that will grab their attention. Research shows that most people will read only the headline, and if it doesn't provide the intrigue necessary to get them to keep reading, then you've lost them before you get to the first sentence.

Remember the psychology behind successful headlines. The goal of a headline is to get the reader to take the next step, whether that means reading your blog, clicking your ad, or filling out a form. Some of the things that can help make headlines intriguing include: surprise, negative superlatives, numbers, curiosity, specificity, and addressing the audience directly.

Good persuasive writing is clean and easy to read. Adjectives can be powerful, but don't overuse them. You're better off using verbs that put a strong visual image in your reader's mind. For example, use trudge, skip, or sidle instead of walk. A conversational style – including addressing your customer directly by using "you" – makes for readable content that will keep customers engaged.

Personalized emails are more likely to be read than emails that aren't personalized. Remember to use psychological principles such as the Rhyme-as-Reason Effect, the Fluency Heuristic, the Bizarreness Effect, scarcity and reverse psychology to keep your email interesting.

Remember that the layout of your emails is just as important as the content. Emails with plenty of white space and good margins, as well as indentations and subheadings, are less fatiguing to read and easier to comprehend.

On your website, try creating a common enemy, creating a fear of missing out, or offering immediate gratification to your customers.

And finally, remember that your calls to action should arouse curiosity or anticipation, or serve as the climax of a story.

The Psychology of Paid Advertising

Paid advertising is a cornerstone of many online marketing strategies, and psychology plays an important role. Some marketers pick the keywords they think are best without taking their customers into consideration. That's a mistake. Always remember that every keyword is a question. People who type keywords into search engines aren't browsing the web; they're looking for specific information. Make sure to take linguistic differences such as regional vocabularies and gender preferences into account when you are selecting keywords.

Remember that your keyword, ad, and website all exist on a continuum. The keyword is a question, the ad is the answer to the question, and your website is either a more detailed answer or a solution.

Headlines are hugely important in paid advertising. Your headline is what's going to convince people to click on your ad and visit your landing page. If it doesn't grab their attention, you might as well save your money.

Images and other visual content can be a good way to draw customers in, both in your paid advertisements and in things like marketing emails. It's important not to limit yourself to one kind of content. Visual can mean many things, and all of them can be appealing to your customers. Consider things like photographs, videos, graphs, charts, infographics, and even comics. Remember, the reptilian brain loves visuals!

Remarketing campaigns are a very effective way of getting customers to finish what they started on your website. Some of the ways to draw them back are to introduce novelty, give them a justification to return, get them to give you a small "Yes" as a precursor to giving a bigger one, and finding a way to reduce the pain of payment.

When you advertise on social media, make use of the rich psychographics to target your ads at specific customer personas.

Finally, remember that every form of paid advertising should include a clear and compelling call to action. People are expecting to see one when they click on an ad or email, and it's important to fulfill customer expectations. While it is important not to focus too much on your product's features, it's not a good idea to be overly coy in your marketing content. The purpose of your ad, email, or website is to convert customers. If you don't tell them what to do, they might not know what to do.

The Psychology of Social Media Marketing

Finally, we come to social media marketing. In many ways, using social media brings everything we've talked about together. Certainly, anyone who's spent time on Facebook and Twitter knows that the majority of people are exceedingly self-centered in what they post. The overwhelming majority of status updates and Tweets are about personal experiences and emotions. That means that social media is the ideal place to focus on your customers and put the psychological principles you've used to work.

One of the key things to remember about social media marketing is that you've got to pick the right platforms for your business. That means knowing who your customers are and where they're likely to be. If you're selling business-to-business, you might want to be on Facebook, but you need to be on LinkedIn. Companies selling aspirational products, especially products that appeal to women, would be foolish to pass up the opportunity to use Pinterest as a marketing tool. Do research to determine which social media sites make sense for your company, and then use them in a way that takes advantage of the site's particular dynamic.

Remember the reasons that most people use social media. They're not using it to get repeated sales pitches from companies – even companies they like. What they want is to feel a sense of community, to give and receive feedback and opinions, to feel better about themselves, and to form a view of the world around them. When it comes to following companies, they're hoping for personal interaction and better customer service. If you're always asking your followers to buy something, you're missing the point.

Your brand has a personality, and your social media pages – everything from your bio to your profile picture to the content you create and share – has to reflect it. Remember the examples from Red Bull and Roll-Royce? Nobody would ever confuse their content, even if you eliminated the brand names. Red Bull uses a casual, irreverent, and brash tone that perfectly mirrors the way people think of their brand. Rolls Royce, on the other hand, uses an elevated and slightly aloof tone that speaks to the fact that they offer a luxury, personalized product that very few people can afford.

Emotions on social media are contagious, and positive emotions are especially so. To encourage people to interact and share your content, maintain a positive tone. It's also a good idea to do everything you can to foster a sense of community and encourage customers to interact. Responding to both positive and negative comments can improve customers' perception of you. And don't forget that participating in charitable giving and talking about on social media can help give your reputation a boost.

Customers First

Digital Marketing is all about your customers. Regardless of what product or service you sell, you can't put together an effective digital marketing campaign if you aren't always focused on your customers. Knowing who they are and what they want will help you accomplish exactly what you want to do. If you lose sight of their importance, you won't be able to persuade them to buy your product or service.

That's the benefit of applying psychological principles to your digital marketing efforts. Every sale you make is a result of a customer's decision – and psychology is what drives those decisions.

APPENDIX

Introduction

1. Neurons & Synapses - Memory & the Brain - The Human Memory. (n.d.). Retrieved August 30, 2015, from http://www.human-memory.net/brain_neurons.html

2. Toro, R., Fox, P. T., & Paus, T. (2008). Functional coactivation map of the human brain. *Cerebral cortex*, *18*(11), 2553-2559.

3. Brain Facts: 10 Mind-Blowing Facts About The Brain - ODDEE. (2012, July 3). Retrieved August 30, 2015, from http://www.oddee.com/item_98246.aspx

4. Brain Facts: 10 Mind-Blowing Facts About The Brain - ODDEE. (2012, July 3). Retrieved August 30, 2015, from http://www.oddee.com/item_98246.aspx

5. 10 Important Differences Between Brains and Computers. (n.d.). Retrieved August 30, 2015.

6. Langer, E. J., Blank, A., & Chanowitz, B. (1978). The mindlessness of ostensibly thoughtful action: The role of" placebic" information in interpersonal interaction. *Journal of personality and social psychology*, *36*(6), 635.

7. Polman, E. (2010). Information distortion in self-other decision making. *Journal of Experimental Social Psychology*, *46*(2), 432-435.

8. Ross, L. (1977). The intuitive psychologist and his shortcomings: Distortions in the attribution process. *Advances in experimental social psychology, 10*, 173-220.

Psychology of Marketing

9. MacLean, P. D. (1990). *The triune brain in evolution: Role in paleocerebral functions.* Springer Science & Business Media.

10. Renvoisé, P., & Morin, C. (2007). *Neuromarketing: Understanding the "buy button" in your customer's brain.* Nashville, Tenn: T. Nelson.

11. Renvoisé, P., & Morin, C. (2007). *Neuromarketing: Understanding the "buy button" in your customer's brain.* Nashville, Tenn: T. Nelson.

12. Renvoisé, P., & Morin, C. (2007). *Neuromarketing: Understanding the "buy button" in your customer's brain.* Nashville, Tenn: T. Nelson.

13. Wilson, T. D., & Gilbert, D. T. (2005). Affective forecasting knowing what to want. *Current Directions in Psychological Science, 14*(3), 131-134.

14. Zhang, T., & Zhang, D. (2007). Agent-based simulation of consumer purchase decision-making and the decoy effect. *Journal of Business Research, 60*(8), 912-922.

15. Goidel, R. K., & Shields, T. G. (1994). The vanishing marginals, the bandwagon, and the mass media. *The Journal of Politics, 56*(03), 802-810.

16. Nielsen, J. (2010, April 6). Nielsen Norman Group. Retrieved August 1, 2015, from http://www.nngroup.com/articles/horizontal-attention-leans-left/

Conversion Rate Optimization

17. Cialdini, R. (2007). *Influence: The psychology of persuasion* (Rev. ed. ; 1st Collins business essentials ed.). New York: Collins.

18. Regan, D. T. (1971). Effects of a favor and liking on compliance. *Journal of Experimental Social Psychology, 7*(6), 627-639.

19. Charities get a generous return from 'freemiums' (n.d.). Retrieved July 24, 2015, from http://www.csmonitor.com/2007/1119/p13s02-wmgn.html

20. Moriarty, T. (1975). Crime, commitment, and the responsive bystander: Two field experiments. *Journal of Personality and Social Psychology, 31*(2), 370.

21. Sherif, M. (1936). The psychology of social norms.

22. Inventor Sylvan Goldman Biography. (n.d.). Retrieved July 24, 2015, from http://www.ideafinder.com/history/inventors/goldman.htm

23. Milgram, S. (1963). Behavioral study of obedience. *The Journal of Abnormal and Social Psychology, 67*(4), 371.

24. Dion, K., Berscheid, E., & Walster, E. (1972). What is beautiful is good. *Journal of personality and social psychology, 24*(3), 285.

25. Brock, T. C. (1965). Communicator-recipient similarity and decision change. *Journal of Personality and Social Psychology, 1*(6), 650.

26. Martin, D. D., & Wilson, J. L. (2012). Apple-polishers, ass-kissers and suck-ups: Towards a sociology of ingratiation. *The Qualitative Report, 17*(34), 1-19.

27. PRELEC, D. (2003). "COHERENT ARBITRARINESS": STABLE DEMAND CURVES WITHOUT STABLE PREFERENCES* DAN ARIELY GEORGE LOEWENSTEIN. *Technology, 73.*

28. Tversky, A., & Kahneman, D. (1981). The framing of decisions and the psychology of choice. *Science, 211*(4481), 453-458.

29. Hasher, L., Goldstein, D., & Toppino, T. (1977). Frequency and the conference of referential validity. *Journal of Verbal Learning and Verbal Behavior, 16*(1), 107-112.

30. Von Restorff, H. (1933). Über die wirkung von bereichsbildungen im spurenfeld. *Psychologische Forschung, 18*(1), 299-342.

31. Iyengar, S. S., & Lepper, M. R. (2000). When choice is demotivating: Can one desire too much of a good thing?. *Journal of personality and social psychology*, *79*(6), 995.

The Psychology of Web Design

32. Sillence, E., Briggs, P., Harris, P., & Fishwick, L. (2007). Health websites that people can trust–the case of hypertension. *Interacting with Computers*, *19*(1), 32-42.

33. Maslow, A. H. (1943). A theory of human motivation. *Psychological review*, *50*(4), 370.

34. Bradley, S. (2010, April 25). Designing For A Hierarchy Of Needs – Smashing Magazine. Retrieved August 30, 2015, from http://www.smashingmagazine.com/2010/04/designing-for-a-hierarchy-of-needs/

35. Nielsen, J. (2006, April 17). Nielsen Norman Group. Retrieved August 1, 2015, from http://www.nngroup.com/articles/f-shaped-pattern-reading-web-content/

36. Nielsen, J. Nielsen, J. (2000, November 12). Nielsen Norman Group. Retrieved August 1, 2015, from http://www.nngroup.com/articles/drop-down-menus-use-sparingly/

37. Nielsen, J. (2010, April 6). Nielsen Norman Group. Retrieved August 1, 2015, from http://www.nngroup.com/articles/horizontal-attention-leans-left/

38. Newman, E. J., Garry, M., Bernstein, D. M., Kantner, J., & Lindsay, D. S. (2012). Nonprobative photographs (or words) inflate truthiness. *Psychonomic bulletin & review*, *19*(5), 969-974.

39. Knutson, B., Wimmer, G. E., Kuhnen, C. M., & Winkielman, P. (2008). Nucleus accumbens activation mediates the influence of reward cues on financial risk taking. *NeuroReport*, *19*(5), 509-513.

40. Ebbinghaus, H. (1913). *Memory: A contribution to experimental psychology* (No. 3). University Microfilms.

41. Bottomley, P. A., & Doyle, J. R. (2006). The interactive effects of colors and products on perceptions of brand logo appropriateness. *Marketing Theory*, *6*(1), 63-83.

42. Hallock, J. (2003). Colour assignment.

43. Auster, C. J., & Mansbach, C. S. (2012). The gender marketing of toys: An analysis of color and type of toy on the Disney store website. *Sex Roles*, *67*(7-8), 375-388.

44. Gendelman, V. (2015, February 17). Font Psychology: How Typefaces Hack Our Brains. Retrieved August 8, 2015, from http://www.companyfolders.com/blog/font-psychology-how-typefaces-hack-our-brains

45. Galfano, G., Dalmaso, M., Marzoli, D., Pavan, G., Coricelli, C., & Castelli, L. (2012). Eye gaze cannot be ignored (but neither can arrows). *The Quarterly Journal of Experimental Psychology*, *65*(10), 1895-1910.

The Psychology of Persuasive Writing

46. The rational and attentive news consumer - American Press Institute. (2014, March 17). Retrieved August 27, 2015.

47. Garfinkel, D. (2006). *Advertising Headlines That Make You Rich: Create Winning Ads, Web Pages, Sales Letters and More*. Morgan James Publishing.

48. Bly, Robert W. *The Copywriter's Handbook: A Step-by-step Guide to Writing Copy That Sells*. New York: Henry Holt, 2005. Print.

49. Ainslie, G., & Haslam, N. (1992). Hyperbolic discounting.

50. Ariely, Dan. *Predictably Irrational: The Hidden Forces That Shape Our Decisions*. New York: Harper Perennial, 2010. Print.

51. Heath, C., & Heath, D. (2007). *Made to stick: Why some ideas survive and others die*. Random House.

52. Berns, G. S., McClure, S. M., Pagnoni, G., & Montague, P. R. (2001). Predictability modulates human brain response to reward. *The Journal of Neuroscience, 21*(8), 2793-2798.

53. Bennett, A. (2013, July 23). Outbrain | Headlines: When the Best Brings the Worst and the Worst Brings the Best. Retrieved August 27, 2015.

54. Ito, T. A., Larsen, J. T., Smith, N. K., & Cacioppo, J. T. (1998). Negative information weighs more heavily on the brain: the negativity bias in evaluative categorizations. *Journal of personality and social psychology, 75*(4), 887.

55. Safran, N. (2013, July 17). 5 Data Insights into the Headlines Readers Click. Retrieved August 27, 2015.

56. Pelham, B. W., Sumarta, T. T., & Myaskovsky, L. (1994). The easy path from many to much: The numerosity heuristic. *Cognitive Psychology, 26*(2), 103-133.

57. Loewenstein, G. (1994). The psychology of curiosity: A review and reinterpretation. *Psychological bulletin, 116*(1), 75.

58. Gruber, M. J., Gelman, B. D., & Ranganath, C. (2014). States of curiosity modulate hippocampus-dependent learning via the dopaminergic circuit. *Neuron, 84*(2), 486-496.

59. Ellsberg, D. (1961). Risk, ambiguity, and the Savage axioms. *The quarterly journal of economics*, 643-669.

60. Lai, L., & Farbrot, A. (2014). What makes you click? The effect of question headlines on readership in computer-mediated communication. *Social Influence, 9*(4), 289-299.

61. Renvoisé, P., & Morin, C. (2007). *Neuromarketing: Understanding the "buy button" in your customer's brain.* Nashville, Tenn: T. Nelson.

62. McGlone, M. S., & Tofighbakhsh, J. (1999). The Keats heuristic: Rhyme as reason in aphorism interpretation. *Poetics, 26*(4), 235-244.

63. Jacoby, L. L., & Dallas, M. (1981). On the relationship between autobiographical memory and perceptual learning. *Journal of Experimental Psychology: General, 110*(3), 306.

64. McDaniel, M. A., & Einstein, G. O. (1986). Bizarre imagery as an effective memory aid: The importance of distinctiveness. *Journal of Experimental Psychology: Learning, Memory, and Cognition, 12*(1), 54.

65. Macklin, C., & McDaniel, M. (2005). The bizarreness effect: Dissociation between item and source memory. *Memory, 13*(7), 682-689.

66. Murdock Jr, B. B. (1962). The serial position effect of free recall. *Journal of experimental psychology, 64*(5), 482.

67. Von Restorff, H. (1933). Über die wirkung von bereichsbildungen im spurenfeld. *Psychologische Forschung, 18*(1), 299-342.

68. Sherif, M. (1936). The psychology of social norms.

69. Van Herpen, E., Pieters, R., & Zeelenberg, M. (2014). When less sells more or less: The scarcity principle in wine choice. *Food Quality and Preference, 36*, 153-160.

70. Brehm, J. W. (1966). A theory of psychological reactance.

71. Chaparro, B., Baker, J. R., Shaikh, A. D., Hull, S., & Brady, L. (2004). Reading online text: A comparison of four whitespace layouts. *Usability News*, *6*(2), 1-7.

72. Chaparro, B. S., Shaikh, A. D., & Baker, J. R. (2005). Reading Online Text with a Poor Layout: Is Performance Worse?. *Usability News*, *7*(1), 1-4.

73. Zviran, M., Te'eni, D., & Gross, Y. (2006). Does color in email make a difference?. *Communications of the ACM*, *49*(4), 94-99.

74. Valdez, P., & Mehrabian, A. (1994). Effects of color on emotions. *Journal of Experimental Psychology: General*, *123*(4), 394.

75. Rettie, R. (2002). Email marketing: success factors.

76. Sullivan, D., Landau, M. J., & Rothschild, Z. K. (2010). An existential function of enemyship: evidence that people attribute influence to personal and political enemies to compensate for threats to control. *Journal of Personality and Social Psychology*, *98*(3), 434.

77. Walton, G. M., Cohen, G. L., Cwir, D., & Spencer, S. J. (2012). Mere belonging: the power of social connections. *Journal of personality and social psychology*, *102*(3), 513.

78. Mischel, W., & Ebbesen, E. B. (1970). Attention in delay of gratification. *Journal of Personality and Social Psychology, 16*(2), 329.

79. Freud, S., & Freud, A. (2001). *Complete psychological works of Sigmund Freud* (Vol. 1). Random House.

80. Renvoisé, P., & Morin, C. (2007). *Neuromarketing: Understanding the "buy button" in your customer's brain.* Nashville, Tenn: T. Nelson.

81. Glen, J., & Walker, R. (n.d.). Significant Objects. Retrieved August 28, 2015, from http://significantobjects. com/experimental-results/

82. Hardy, M., & Heyes, S. (1999). *Beginning psychology.* Oxford University Press.

83. Smith, A. A., Malmo, R. B., & Shagass, C. (1954). An electromyographic study of listening and talking. *Canadian Journal of Psychology/Revue canadienne de psychologie, 8*(4), 219.

84. MacLeod, A. K., & Byrne, A. (1996). Anxiety, depression, and the anticipation of future positive and negative experiences. *Journal of abnormal psychology, 105*(2), 286.

85. Bianchi, C. (2011). Semiotic approaches to advertising texts and strategies: Narrative, passion, marketing. *Semiotica, 2011*(183), 243-271.

86. Pavlov, I. P., & Anrep, G. V. E. (1960). *Conditioned Reflexes: An Investigation of the Physiological Activity of the Cerebral Cortex; Translated [from the Russian] and Edited by GV Anrep*. Dover Publications.

The Psychology of Paid Advertising

87. Geddes, B. (2014). *Advanced Google AdWords*. John Wiley & Sons, 8-9.

88. Geddes, B. (2014). *Advanced Google AdWords*. John Wiley & Sons, 9-11.

89. Words Known by Men and Women. (2014, June 13). Retrieved August 29, 2015, from http://gnodevel.ugent. be/crr.ugent.be/archives/1628

90. Geddes, B. (2014). *Advanced Google AdWords*. John Wiley & Sons, 26-27.

91. Douglas, L., & Connor, R. (2003). Attitudes to service quality-the expectation gap. *Nutrition & Food Science*, *33*(4), 165-172.

92. Kent, R. J., & Allen, C. T. (1994). Competitive interference effects in consumer memory for advertising: the role of brand familiarity. *The Journal of Marketing*, 97-105.

93. Aloisi, A. M., Casamenti, F., Scali, C., Pepeu, G., & Carli, G. (1997). Effects of novelty, pain and stress on

hippocampal extracellular acetylcholine levels in male rats. *Brain Research, 748*(1), 219-226.

94. Bunzeck, N., & Düzel, E. (2006). Absolute coding of stimulus novelty in the human substantia nigra/VTA. *Neuron, 51*(3), 369-379.

95. Cohen, J. B., & Goldberg, M. E. (1970). The dissonance model in post-decision product evaluation. *Journal of Marketing Research*, 315-321.

96. Robinson, P. H., & Darley, J. M. (1998). Testing competing theories of justification. *North Carolina Law Review, 76*, 1095-1143.

97. Dickens, C. (2000). *A Tale of Two Cities*. Penguin.

98. Ruvio, A., Gavish, Y., & Shoham, A. (2013). Consumer's doppelganger: A role model perspective on intentional consumer mimicry. *Journal of Consumer Behaviour, 12*(1), 60-69.

99. Ellsberg, D. (1961). Risk, ambiguity, and the Savage axioms. *The quarterly journal of economics*, 643-669.

100. Knox, R. E., & Inkster, J. A. (1968). POSTDECISION DISSONANCE AT POST TIME1.

101. Freedman, J. L., & Fraser, S. C. (1966). Compliance without pressure: the foot-in-the-door technique. *Journal of personality and social psychology, 4*(2), 195.

102. Knutson, B., Rick, S., Wimmer, G. E., Prelec, D., & Loewenstein, G. (2007). Neural predictors of purchases. *Neuron, 53*(1), 147-156.

103. Kivetz, R., Urminsky, O., & Zheng, Y. (2006). The goal-gradient hypothesis resurrected: Purchase acceleration, illusionary goal progress, and customer retention. *Journal of Marketing Research, 43*(1), 39-58.

104. Weber, S., Witt, S. F., & Moutinho, L. (1989). Psychographic segmentation. *Tourism marketing and management handbook.*, 341-344.

105. Tuškej, U., Golob, U., & Podnar, K. (2013). The role of consumer–brand identification in building brand relationships. *Journal of Business Research, 66*(1), 53-59.

The Psychology of Social Media

106. Hofmann, W., Baumeister, R. F., Förster, G., & Vohs, K. D. (2012). Everyday temptations: an experience sampling study of desire, conflict, and self-control. *Journal of personality and social psychology, 102*(6), 1318.

107. Barraza, J. A., & Zak, P. J. (2009). Empathy toward strangers triggers oxytocin release and subsequent generosity. *Annals of the New York Academy of Sciences, 1167*(1), 182-189.

108. Neumann, I. D. (2008). Brain oxytocin: a key regulator of emotional and social behaviours in both females and males. *Journal of neuroendocrinology*, *20*(6), 858-865.

109. Social networking sites and our lives. (2011, June 15). Retrieved August 30, 2015.

110. Gonzales, A. L., & Hancock, J. T. (2011). Mirror, mirror on my Facebook wall: Effects of exposure to Facebook on self-esteem. *Cyberpsychology, Behavior, and Social Networking*, *14*(1-2), 79-83.

111. Berger, J., & Milkman, K. L. (2012). What makes online content viral?. *Journal of marketing research*, *49*(2), 192-205.

112. Rosen, L. (2012, July 15). The Power of "Like" Retrieved August 30, 2015.

113. Echterhoff, G., Higgins, E. T., & Groll, S. (2005). Audience-tuning effects on memory: the role of shared reality. *Journal of personality and social psychology*, *89*(3), 257.

114. Hamilton, R., Vohs, K. D., & McGill, A. L. (2014). We'll Be Honest, This Won't Be the Best Article You'll Ever Read: The Use of Dispreferred Markers in Word-of-Mouth Communication. *Journal of Consumer Research*, *41*(1), 197-212.

115. Shrauger, J. S., & Schoeneman, T. J. (1979). Symbolic interactionist view of self-concept: Through the looking glass darkly. *Psychological Bulletin, 86*(3), 549.

116. Zhao, S. (2005). The digital self: Through the looking glass of telecopresent others. *Symbolic Interaction, 28*(3), 387-405.

117. Kalyanaraman, S., & Ivory, J. (2006). The face of online information processing: Effects of emoticons on impression formation, affect, and cognition in chat transcripts. In *56th annual convention of the International Communication Association (ICa), Dresden, Germany.*

118. Tchokni, S., Séaghdha, D. O., & Quercia, D. (2014, May). Emoticons and phrases: Status symbols in social media. In *Eighth International AAAI Conference on Weblogs and Social Media.*

119. Toma, C. L., & Hancock, J. T. (2013). Self-affirmation underlies Facebook use. *Personality and Social Psychology Bulletin, 39*(3), 321-331.

120. Wildschut, T., Sedikides, C., Arndt, J., & Routledge, C. (2006). Nostalgia: content, triggers, functions. *Journal of personality and social psychology, 91*(5), 975.

121. Carmon, Z., & Ariely, D. (2000). Focusing on the forgone: How value can appear so different to buyers and sellers. *Journal of Consumer Research, 27*(3), 360-370.

122. Coviello, Lorenzo, et al, "Detecting Emotional Contagion in Massive Social Networks", March 12, 2014, web

123. Lewis, Tanya, "Emotions Can Be Contagious on Online Social Networks", July 1, 2014, web

124. Todorov, Alexander, "Misleading First Impressions", May 27, 2014. Web

125. Tobin, Stephanie J. et al., "Threats to Belonging on Facebook: Lurking and Ostracism", March 7, 2014, web

126. Berger, J., & Milkman, K. L. (2013). Emotion and virality: what makes online content go viral?. *GfK Marketing Intelligence Review, 5*(1), 18-23.

127. Carmon, Z., & Ariely, D. (2000). Focusing on the forgone: How value can appear so different to buyers and sellers. *Journal of Consumer Research, 27*(3), 360-370.

128. Asch, S. E. (1956). Studies of independence and conformity: I. A minority of one against a unanimous majority. *Psychological monographs: General and applied, 70*(9), 1.

129. Wang, X., Yu, C., & Wei, Y. (2012). Social media peer communication and impacts on purchase intentions: A consumer socialization framework. *Journal of Interactive Marketing, 26*(4), 198-208.

130. Zajonc, R. B. (1968). Attitudinal effects of mere exposure. *Journal of personality and social psychology, 9*(2p2), 1.

131. Festinger, L., Back, K. W., & Schachter, S. (1950). *Social pressures in informal groups: A study of human factors in housing* (No. 3). Stanford University Press.

132. Crnic, K. A., Greenberg, M. T., Ragozin, A. S., Robinson, N. M., & Basham, R. B. (1983). Effects of stress and social support on mothers and premature and full-term infants. *Child development*, 209-217.

133. Mar, R. A., & Oatley, K. (2008). The function of fiction is the abstraction and simulation of social experience. *Perspectives on psychological science*, *3*(3), 173-192.

CPSIA information can be obtained
at www.ICGtesting.com
Printed in the USA
LVHW021005081019
633523LV00016B/1657/P

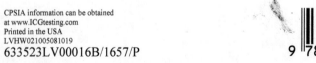

9 780994 390226